World Wisdom
The Library of Perennial Philosophy

The Library of Perennial Philosophy is dedicated to the exposition of the timeless Truth underlying the diverse religions. This Truth, often referred to as the *Sophia Perennis*—or Perennial Wisdom—finds its expression in the revealed Scriptures as well as the writings of the great sages and the artistic creations of the traditional worlds.

To Have a Center appears as one of our selections in the Writings of Frithjof Schuon series.

The Writings of Frithjof Schuon

The Writings of Frithjof Schuon form the foundation of our library because he is the pre-eminent exponent of the Perennial Philosophy. His work illuminates this perspective in both an essential and comprehensive manner like none other.

English Language Writings of Frithjof Schuon

Original Books

The Transcendent Unity of Religions
Spiritual Perspectives and Human Facts
Gnosis: Divine Wisdom
Language of the Self
Stations of Wisdom
Understanding Islam
Light on the Ancient Worlds
Treasures of Buddhism (In the Tracks of Buddhism)
Logic and Transcendence
Esoterism as Principle and as Way
Castes and Races
Sufism: Veil and Quintessence
From the Divine to the Human
Christianity/Islam: Essays on Esoteric Ecumenicism
Survey of Metaphysics and Esoterism
In the Face of the Absolute
The Feathered Sun: Plains Indians in Art and Philosophy
To Have a Center
Roots of the Human Condition
Images of Primordial and Mystic Beauty: Paintings by Frithjof Schuon
Echoes of Perennial Wisdom
The Play of Masks
Road to the Heart: Poems
The Transfiguration of Man
The Eye of the Heart
Form and Substance in the Religions
Adastra & Stella Maris: Poems by Frithjof Schuon (bilingual edition)
Autumn Leaves & The Ring: Poems by Frithjof Schuon (bilingual edition)
Songs without Names, Volumes I-VI: Poems by Frithjof Schuon
Songs without Names, Volumes VII-XII: Poems by Frithjof Schuon
World Wheel, Volumes I-III: Poems by Frithjof Schuon
World Wheel, Volumes IV-VII: Poems by Frithjof Schuon
Primordial Meditation: Contemplating the Real

Edited Writings

The Essential Frithjof Schuon, ed. Seyyed Hossein Nasr
Songs for a Spiritual Traveler: Selected Poems (bilingual edition)
René Guénon: Some Observations, ed. William Stoddart
The Fullness of God: Frithjof Schuon on Christianity,
ed. James S. Cutsinger
Prayer Fashions Man: Frithjof Schuon on the Spiritual Life,
ed. James S. Cutsinger
Art from the Sacred to the Profane: East and West,
ed. Catherine Schuon
Splendor of the True: A Frithjof Schuon Reader,
ed. James S. Cutsinger

To Have a Center

A New Translation with Selected Letters

by

Frithjof Schuon

Includes Other Previously Unpublished Writings

Edited by

Harry Oldmeadow

To Have a Center:
A New Translation with Selected Letters

Translated by Mark Perry and Jean-Pierre Lafouge

Published in French as
Avoir un Centre,
Éditions Maisonneuve & Larose, 1988,
L'Harmattan, 2010

Library of Congress Cataloging-in-Publication Data

Schuon, Frithjof, 1907-1998.
[Avoir un centre. English]
To have a center : a new translation with selected letters / by Frithjof Schuon ; edited by Harry Oldmeadow.
pages cm. -- (The writings of Frithjof Schuon) (World Wisdom : the library of perennial philosophy)
"Includes other previously unpublished writings."
Includes bibliographical references and index.
ISBN 978-1-936597-44-4 (pbk. : alk. paper) 1. Metaphysics. 2. Human beings. 3. Religion--Philosophy. I. Oldmeadow, Harry, 1947- editor. II. Title.
BD112.S22 2015
110--dc23

2015007471

Cover:
The Medieval Universe,
after a French manuscript of the fourteenth century.
Paris, Bibliothèque Nationale.

Printed on acid-free paper in the United States of America

For information address World Wisdom, Inc.
P.O. Box 2682, Bloomington, Indiana 47402-2682
www.worldwisdom.com

CONTENTS

EDITOR'S PREFACE

As the essay "To Have a Center" opens the present work and deals directly with "the ambiguous possibility that is genius" (p. 10), let us state unequivocally that Frithjof Schuon was himself a man of genius. His exalted intellectual powers were made manifest primarily in his masterly metaphysical writings, but also in his poetry and painting—a genius that was at the same time analytic, speculative, synthetic, and creative. Schuon himself remarks that

> we live in a world which on the one hand tends to deprive men of their center, and on the other hand offers them—in place of the saint and the hero—the cult of the "genius"; now a genius is all too often a man without a center, in whom this lack is replaced by a creative hypertrophy. Certainly, there is a genius proper to normal, hence balanced and virtuous, man; but the world of "culture" and "art for art's sake" accepts with the same enthusiasm normal and abnormal men, the latter being particularly numerous . . . in that world of dreams or nightmares that was the nineteenth century (p. 7).

In contrast to most of the "geniuses" heralded by the modern world, Schuon stands almost alone in exemplifying "a genius proper to normal, hence balanced and virtuous, man"—such as we find in earlier times in a Virgil, a Dante, or a Fra Angelico. It is a sure sign of the times that Schuon's genius remains largely unrecognized today.

Schuon's writings are concerned with the elucidation of timeless metaphysical and cosmological principles and, in their light, the explication of the various and manifold forms—doctrinal, ritual, ethical, artistic—in which these principles find concrete expression in traditional civilizations. In the main our author does not concern himself with the particularities of either the vagaries of history or the cultural aberrations of modernity. He is not captive to that historicist frame of mind which imagines that everything is to be explained in terms of its temporal development. However, as he observes, the subject of the opening essay obliges him to depart from his normal practice; after a brief overview of the normative spiritual anthropology of India, he focuses on the humanistic culture that characterizes modernity, particularly its nineteenth century expressions. It is, fundamentally, a culture of negation:

> Humanistic culture, insofar as it functions as an ideology and therefore as a religion, consists essentially in ignoring three things: firstly, what God is, because it does not accord primacy to Him; secondly, what man is, because it puts him in place of God; thirdly, what the meaning of life is, because this culture limits itself to playing with evanescent things and to plunging into them with criminal unconsciousness (p. 29).

These denials and betrayals are on full display in the culture of post-medieval Europe. Now, Schuon elsewhere readily concedes that profane genius can, "in any human climate", be "the medium of a cosmic quality, of an archetype of beauty or greatness", in which case we can respect at least some of its fruits even though they lie outside tradition:

> Modern art—starting from the Renaissance—does include some more or less isolated works which, though they fit into the style of their period, are in a deeper sense opposed to it and neutralize its errors by their own qualities.[1]

However, what we witness so often is a "useless profusion of talents and geniuses" driven by a "humanistic narcissism with its mania for individualistic and unlimited production" (p. 8). Schuon goes on to illustrate his theme with reference to the lives and creations of a whole gallery of nineteenth century artists, among them Beethoven, Wagner, Rodin, Nietzsche, Wilde, Gauguin, Van Gogh, Ibsen, Bizet, Balzac, Dickens, Tolstoy, and Dostoevsky—all figures whose prodigious talents were turned astray by an impoverished environment, which is not to deny the traces of beauty and grandeur which can be found in many of their works. That many of these geniuses led unhappy and desperate lives only adds to their prestige and strengthens the "seduction, indeed the fascination, which emanates from their siren

[1] Frithjof Schuon, *Art from the Sacred to the Profane: East and West*, edited by Catherine Schuon (Bloomington, IN: World Wisdom, 2007), p. 15.

songs and tragic destinies" (p. 7). The "unbridled subjectivism" and the "split and heteroclitic psychism" (p. 7) of many of the century's geniuses often induced melancholy and despair, sometimes psychopathology and insanity—all deriving ultimately from that loss of a center which is the very hallmark of modern humanism and which can only be restored by a proper understanding of God, of man, and of the human vocation.

The opening essay commands attention precisely because of its distinctive place in the Schuonian corpus. In the rest of Section I ("Integral Anthropology"), and in Sections II ("Ontology and Cosmology") and III ("Spiritual Perspectives") the author returns to more universal themes and concerns. Mention should perhaps be made of the essay "David, Shankara, Honen", most obviously because Schuon himself belongs in a lineage of metaphysicians which includes the great Indian sage. In a letter written late in his life Schuon remarks, "Being *a priori* a metaphysician, I have had since my youth a particular interest in *Advaita Vedānta*, but also in the spiritual method of realization of which the *Advaita Vedānta* approves".[2] In another letter Schuon writes, "Three spiritual beacons for me are Shankara, Honen, and David: Shankara for metaphysics; Honen for the invocation; and David for prayer" (p. 152). This stands as a salutary reminder that Schuon's metaphysical and philosophical concerns are never divorced from the imperatives of the spiritual life itself. Section IV ("Various Subjects") comprises three fascinating excursions into apparently localized subjects whose relationship to metaphysical principles might at first seem tenuous, even remote: the art of translation, the "vestimentary art" of the American Plains Indians (with whom the author felt a profound affinity), and the astronomical systems of Ptolemy and Copernicus; but, as the author remarks, "in spirituality everything is related" (p. ix).

—— ·:· ——

[2] From a letter of January 1996, quoted in the editor's Introduction to *Prayer Fashions Man: Frithjof Schuon on the Spiritual Life*, selected and edited by James S. Cutsinger (Bloomington, IN: World Wisdom, 2005), p. xviii.

To Have a Center

These essays first appeared in French in 1988 as *Avoir un Centre* (Paris: Maisonneuve & Larose);[3] the first English translation by Gustavo Polit was published in 1990 (Bloomington: World Wisdom). The present fully revised translation by Mark Perry and Jean-Pierre Lafouge is the latest in the World Wisdom series of fresh translations of Schuon's works, each including extensive editorial annotations and a full glossary of foreign words and phrases. Like the other volumes in the series, it incorporates excerpts from the author's letters and other hitherto unpublished sources; these more intimate and informal writings deepen and enrich the cardinal themes of *To Have a Center*.

Harry Oldmeadow

[3] A more recent French edition (Paris: L'Harmattan) was published in 2010.

FOREWORD

Quite paradoxically, it is sometimes more difficult to find a title than to write a book; one always knows what one wishes to say, but one does not always know what to call it. It is true that the difficulty does not result from the nature of things, for one could follow the example of Rumi and entitle a work "A Book Which Contains What It Contains" (*Kitāb fīhi mā fīhi*); but we live in a world which is little inclined to accept such a defiance of convention and which obliges us to be a bit more intelligibly specific. Thus we shall choose the title of the first chapter: "To Have a Center", which introduces in its way the subsequent chapters, dealing with anthropology at all its levels and also, further on, metaphysics and spiritual life.

There is the order of principles, which is immutable, and the order of information—traditional or otherwise—of which one can say that it is inexhaustible: on the one hand, not everything in this book will be new for our usual readers and, on the other hand, they will nonetheless find here precisions and illustrations which may have their usefulness. One never has too many keys in view of the "one thing needful", however indirect and simple these points of reference may be.

We acknowledge that this volume contains subjects which are very uneven in scope: one will find a chapter on the art of translating, another on vestimentary art, and another still on a question of astronomy. But in spirituality everything is related: one always has the right to project the light of principles onto subjects of minor importance, and it goes without saying that one often is obliged to do so. As the Duke of Orléans said: "All that is national is ours"; which we shall paraphrase by recalling that all that is normally human, hence virtually spiritual, enters *ipso facto* into our perspective; and "it takes all kinds to make a world".

After what we have just said, the question may be asked whether the *sophia perennis* is a "humanism"; the answer could in principle be "yes", but in fact it must be "no" since humanism in the conventional sense of the term *de facto* exalts fallen man and not man as such. The humanism of the modernists is, practically speaking, a utilitarianism focused on fragmentary man; it is the intention to make oneself as useful as possible to a humanity as useless as possible. As for integral anthropology, we intend, precisely, to give an account of it in the present book.

Frithjof Schuon in 1974

I.

INTEGRAL ANTHROPOLOGY

1. To Have a Center

To be normal is to be homogeneous, and to be homogeneous is to have a center. A normal man is one whose tendencies are, if not altogether uniform, at least concordant—that is to say, sufficiently concordant to convey that decisive center which we may call the sense of the Absolute or the love of God. The tendency towards the Absolute, for which we are made, is difficult to realize in a heterogeneous soul—a soul lacking a center, precisely, and by that fact contrary to its reason for being. Such a soul is *a priori* a "house divided against itself", thus destined to collapse, eschatologically speaking.

The anthropology of India—which is spiritual as well as social—distinguishes on the one hand between homogeneous men whose centers are situated at three different levels,[1] and on the other hand between these men taken as a totality and those who, having no center, are not homogeneous;[2] it attributes this lack either to a degeneration or to a "mixture of castes"—especially those castes that are furthest removed from each other. But it is of the natural castes, not the social ones, that we wish to speak here: the former do not always coincide with the castes representing them socially, for the institutional caste allows for exceptions, inasmuch as it becomes numerically very large and thereby includes all human possibilities. Thus, without wanting to concern ourselves with the castes of India, we shall describe as succinctly as possible the fundamental tendencies which they are meant to transmit, tendencies which are found wherever there are men, with various predominant traits according to the nature of the group.

There is first of all the intellective, speculative, contemplative, sacerdotal type, which tends towards wisdom or holiness—holiness referring more particularly to contemplation, and wisdom to discernment. Next there is the warlike and royal type, which tends towards glory and heroism; even in spirituality—since holiness is for everyone—this type will readily be active and heroic, whence the ideal of the "heroicalness of virtues". The third type is the "honorably average" man: he is essentially a hard worker, well-balanced, perse-

[1] The *brāhmana*, the *kshatriya*, the *vaishya*.

[2] The *shūdra*, the *chandāla* or *panchama*.

vering; his center is love for work that is useful and well done, and carried out with God in mind; he aspires neither to transcendence nor to glory—although he desires to be both pious and respectable—yet he nonetheless shares with the sacerdotal type a love of peace and finds little appeal in adventures; and this predisposes him to a contemplativeness in keeping with his occupations.[3] Lastly there is the type that has no ideal other than more or less gross pleasure; this is lustful man who, not knowing how to control himself, has to be controlled by others, so that his great virtue will be submission and fidelity.

No doubt, the man who finds his center only outside himself—in pleasures, without which he feels like a void—is not really "normal"; but he is nonetheless redeemable through his submission to someone better than he, and who will serve as his center. This in fact is exactly what happens—but on a higher plane which may concern any man—in the relation between disciple and spiritual master.

But there is still another human possibility, namely the man who lacks a center, not because lust deprives him of it, but because he has two or even three centers at once: this is the type known as the pariah,[4] arising from a "mixture of castes", and who bears in himself the double or triple heredity of divergent types: that of the sacerdotal type, for example, combined with the materialistic and hedonistic type of which we have just spoken. This new type—who is unhinged—is capable "of everything and nothing": he is a mimic and a born comedian, always looking for a makeshift center, hence for a psychic homogeneity which can only elude him. The pariah has neither center nor continuity; he is a void eager for sensations; his life is a disconnected series of arbitrary experiences. The danger this type represents for society is evident since one never knows whom one is dealing with; no one is willing to trust a leader who is at bottom a circus showman and one who by his nature is predisposed to crime. This is what explains the ostracism of the Hindu system towards those who, born from too heterogeneous a breeding, are "outcastes". We say that this explains the ostracism, and not that this excuses the abuses,

[3] From the standpoint of "caste" this third type is particularly complex and unequal: it contains in fact peasants, craftsmen, and merchants. Thus, apart from all social classifications, it includes tendencies which may be quite uneven.

[4] A loan word in the European languages, derived from the Tamil *paraiyan*, "tambourine man".

or that the assessment made of individuals is always fair—something which is impossible to do in practice.[5]

Generally speaking, a man's psychological type is a matter, not of the exclusive presence of a given tendency, but of its predominance; and in this sense—or with this reservation—we may say that the first of the types enumerated is "spiritual"; the second, "noble"; the third, "upright"; the fourth, "lustful"; and the fifth, "vain" and "transgressing". Spirituality, nobility, uprightness: these are the fundamental tendencies of men who, according to the Hindu doctrine, are qualified for initiation or "twice born"; lust and vanity: these are the tendencies of those who *a priori* are not concretely qualified for a spiritual path but who, being men, nevertheless have no choice; which amounts to saying that every man can save himself in principle. As Ghazzali said, men have to be driven into Paradise with whips.

Thus there is hope for the man who has no center, whatever the cause of his privation or infirmity may be; for there is a supra-human Center that is always available to us, and whose trace we bear within ourselves, given that we are made in the image of the Creator. That is why Christ could say that what is impossible for man is always possible for God; however decentralized man may be, as soon as he sincerely turns to Heaven his relationship with God bestows a center on him; we are always at the center of the world when we address the Eternal. That is the point of view of the three monotheistic religions of Semitic origin, and also that of human distress and of Divine Mercy.[6]

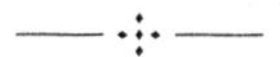

It is crucial not to confuse the absence of a center—which is abnormal—in the hylic and somatic type, with the same absence—but normal in this case and situated on an altogether different plane—in the feminine sex; for it is only too evident that if as a sexual being woman seeks her center in man, she is nonetheless in full possession

[5] The Hindu system sacrifices the exceptional cases in the interest of the collectivity, for the sake of maintaining quality, on the one hand, and the perennial renewal of this quality, on the other.

[6] A point of view which is likewise found in Buddhism and in certain sectors of Hinduism, and necessarily so since human misery is one, just as man is one.

of her center in precisely the respect in which hylics or pariahs do not possess it. In other words: if woman as such aspires to a center situated outside herself, namely, in the complementary sex—just as the latter in the same respect seeks his vital space in his sexual complement—as a human being she nonetheless benefits from an integral personality, on condition that she be humanly in conformity with the norm, which implies the capacity to think objectively, especially in cases where virtue requires it. Too often it is thought that woman is capable of objectivity and thus of disinterested logic only at the expense of her femininity,[7] which is radically false; woman has to realize, not specifically masculine traits of course, but the normatively and primordially human qualities, which are obligatory for every human being; and this is independent of feminine psychology as such.[8]

Another point to be considered is the personal center in connection with certain racial factors. If the mixture between two races too different from each other is to be avoided, it is precisely because this disparity generally has as a consequence that the individual possesses two centers, which means practically speaking that he has none; in other words, that he has no identity. But there are also cases where, on the contrary, the mixture gives rise to a harmonious result, namely when each parent represents a sort of racial supersaturation, such that the racial type is limitative rather than positive; in such cases, the combination with the foreign race appears as a liberation and re-establishes equilibrium; but this solution is as exceptional as are its conditions. Besides, every soul contains two poles, but normally they are complementary and not divergent.

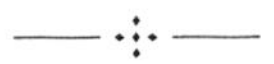

[7] The feminists themselves—of both sexes—are convinced of this, at least implicitly and in practice, otherwise they would not aspire to the virilization of woman.

[8] Legitimate feminine psychology results from the principial prototype of woman—from the universal Substance—as well as from the biological, moral, and social functions which she personifies; and this implies the right to limitations, to weaknesses, if one wishes, but not to defects. A human being is one thing, and the male is another; and it is a great pity that the two things have often been confused even in languages which—like Greek, Latin, and German—make this distinction; a confusion due to the fact that the male is more central than the female, thus also more integral, but this reason has only a relative import, because man (*homo*, not *vir*) is one.

The practical interest of all these considerations lies in the fact that we live in a world which on the one hand tends to deprive men of their center, and on the other hand offers them—in place of the saint and the hero—the cult of the "genius"; now a genius is all too often a man without a center, in whom this lack is replaced by a creative hypertrophy. Certainly, there is a genius proper to normal, hence balanced and virtuous, man; but the world of "culture" and of "art for art's sake" accepts with the same enthusiasm normal and abnormal men, the latter being particularly numerous—to the extent that men of genius can be—in that world of dreams or nightmares that was the nineteenth century. That geniuses of this kind have often been unfortunate and desperate persons who have ended in disaster, does not deprive them of any prestige in public opinion; quite the contrary, people find them all the more interesting and "authentic", and allow themselves to be attracted by the seduction, indeed the fascination, which emanates from their siren songs and tragic destinies.

Let us take the example of a man who has two heredities and thus two equivalent centers, one intellectual and idealistic and another materialistic and pleasure-driven: as an intellectual, this man will forge a philosophy, but it will be determined by his materialism and his love of pleasure; as a materialist, he will enjoy life as a *bon vivant*, but his pleasures will be intellectualized, thus he will enjoy life as an epicurean and an aesthete. And he will be an elusive and inconsistent man, dominated by the pleasure of the moment which he will always justify by his hedonistic philosophy; and this is one of the most lethal possibilities there is.

Consequently it is not astonishing that a man who is at once a man of genius and lacking a true center should easily be a psychopath—and this precisely on account of his unbridled subjectivism—whether he be a schizoid artist, a paranoid politician, or some other such caricature of grandeur. It is all very well to admire the qualities of a brilliant work of art; but its creator may have, alongside his genius, a perfectly odious character; thus the values that are manifested in his creations, or in some of them, pertain only to a single compartment of his split and heteroclitic psychism, and not to a homogeneous personality.

As for profane genius as such, aside from the question of knowing whether it is normal or morbid, good or bad, it is important to know that it can be the medium for a cosmic quality, for an archetype of beauty or grandeur, and in that case it would be unfair to reject its production; but it would likewise be unfair to despise it for the simple reason that it does not pertain to traditional art, just as, conversely, it would be sheer prejudice to admire a work for the sole reason that it is traditional or sacred, since it could be badly executed and manifest unintelligence as well as ineptitude. In short, cosmic values, or aesthetic and moral qualities, can manifest themselves incidentally in any human climate, to the extent that it does not set up an obstacle to them.[9]

One has to insist, therefore, on this point: what is blameworthy in the exteriorized and worldly genius is not necessarily his production, but the fact that he sets his center outside himself, in a work which in a certain manner deprives him of his real core or puts itself in place of it. Such is not the case for genius not determined by humanism: in Dante, for example, or in Virgil, their work was the providential manifestation of an immensely rich and profound center; of a "genius", precisely, but in the ideal, normative, and legitimate sense of the term. The criterion of such genius is that the author is as interested in his salvation as in his work, and that his work bears the trace of this. No doubt—when speaking of literature—this criterion could not appear in each poem or in each tale, but it applies to every work that demands a lengthy reading and has to compensate for this monopolization of our attention by a fragrance that is spiritual and interiorizing. Every writer or artist ought to communicate—in addition to his literal message—if not elements of truth, of nobility, and of virtue, at least eschatological ideas; the most stupid and perverse prejudice being "art for art's sake", which cannot be founded on anything whatsoever.

Indisputably, it is humanistic narcissism with its mania for individualistic and unlimited production that is responsible for this ultimately useless profusion of talents and geniuses. The humanistic perspective

[9] It should be noted that, apart from the superior modes of talent or of genius—modes to which the great musicians and actors belong—there are also cerebral prodigies such as calculators and chess players, or prodigies of imagination and vitality such as the great adventurers; we mention such types here on account of the category of the phenomenon, even though, not producing any works of art, these people remain outside of our subject.

not only proposes the cult of man, but—by that very fact—also aims at perfecting man according to an ideal that does not transcend the human plane. Now, this moral idealism is fruitless because it depends entirely on a human ideology; such an ideal wants man to be ceaselessly productive and dynamic, whence the cult of genius, precisely. The moral ideal of humanism is inefficacious because it is subject to the tastes of the moment, or to fashion, if one wishes;[10] for human qualities, which imply by definition the will to transcend oneself, are not vitally relevant unless connected to something that transcends us. Just as man's reason for being does not lie within man as such, so too man's qualities do not represent an end in themselves; it is not for nothing that deifying gnosis requires the virtues. A quality is fully legitimate only on condition that it derive, in the last analysis, from necessary Being and not from mere contingency, that is to say, not from what is merely possible.

The initial contradiction of humanism is that, if one man can prescribe for himself an ideal that pleases him, so too can someone else, for the same reason, prescribe for himself another ideal, or indeed nothing at all; and in fact amoral humanism is almost as ancient as moralistic humanism.[11] The moralizing candor of a Kant or a Rousseau is followed by the adventurous amoralism of a Nietzsche; people no longer say "humanism is morality", they now say "I am morality"—even when this morality is the absence of all morality.

Voltaire expressed the wish that every man should be "seated under his fig tree, eating his bread without asking himself what is in it"[12] (we quote from memory). He means: sheltered from the tyranny of dogmas and priests; and, good humanist that he is, he completely forgets that the decent fellow he is dreaming of is potentially a savage

[10] The ostentatiously human perfection of classical or academic art has in reality nothing universally convincing about it; this was noticed long ago, but only in order to fall into the contrary excess, namely, the cult of ugliness and of the inhuman, despite a few intermediary oases—certain impressionists, for example. The classicism of a Canova or an Ingres no longer convinces anyone, but that is no reason for acknowledging only Melanesian fetishes.

[11] On the more or less traditionalist side one also speaks of "hominism"—with a reproving intention—no doubt because the term "humanism" still evokes "classical" associations of ideas which one still feels obliged to uphold.

[12] That is to say: without concerning himself with the supernatural, the mysteries, in short with things that are humanly unverifiable.

beast; in other words, that man is not necessarily good, and that the only thing which protects man from man—or the good from the bad— is precisely religion, tyrannical or not. And religion does so even if it unleashes in turn some bad men against some good men, which in any case is inevitable and by far the lesser evil compared to a world without religious discipline, a world delivered into the hands of man alone, precisely.

Since our thesis on the human center has led us to mention the ambiguous possibility that is genius, we shall take the liberty of illustrating our preceding considerations by a few concrete examples, without wishing to plunge into "all too human" (*allzumenschlich*) blind alleys; this is not in keeping with our habit, but our subject more or less obliges us to do so. The reader should not be surprised if, in what follows, he enters as it were into a new world.

A Beethoven, despite being a believer, was inevitably situated on the plane of humanism, hence of "horizontality". And although there was nothing morbid about him, we note the characteristic disproportion between the artistic work and the spiritual personality; characteristic, precisely, for the type of genius arising from the cult of man, thus from the Renaissance and its consequences. There is no denying what is powerful and profound about many of Beethoven's musical motifs, but, all things considered, a music of this sort should not exist; it exteriorizes and thereby exhausts possibilities which ought to remain inward and contribute in their own way to the contemplative scope of the soul.[13] In this sense, Beethoven's art is both an indiscretion and a squandering, as is the case with most post-Renaissance artistic manifestations; [14] even so, compared to certain other geniuses,

[13] It is quite possible that if Ramakrishna had heard the Seventh Symphony and if he could have grasped its musical language, he would have fallen into *samādhi*, something which happened to him when he saw a lion for the first time, or when an Indian dancing girl was brought before him; but we doubt very much that there are many Ramakrishnas among Beethoven's listeners, so the argument has hardly any practical value as regards the spiritual and social justification of such an exteriorized and communicative music, one which is in fact a "two-edged sword".

[14] Whereas in Bach or Mozart musicality still manifests itself with faultless crystallin-

Beethoven was a homogeneous man, hence "normal", if we disregard his demiurgic passion for musical exteriorization.

Alongside motifs possessing all the pure beauty of the archetypes, there are necessarily in Beethoven and his successors—for example in Wagner—features denoting the megalomania of the Renaissance and thus of humanistic idealism. While appreciating particular musical motifs, and different polyphonic harmonies which throw them into relief, one cannot help noticing the disproportionate and "ponderous" side of the musical production in question; a melody may be celestial, but a symphony or an opera is excessive. It should be noted, however, that the great deviation of the *Cinquecento* had much less of an effect on music and poetry than on painting, sculpture, and architecture; thus the megalomaniacal character of this or that modern music refers finally more directly—from the standpoint of affinity—to the plastic arts of the Renaissance rather than to its musical arts.[15]

Having spoken of music, let us pass on to another example of creations of genius, this time of a visual character but equally powerful and quasi-volcanic: namely Rodin, direct heir to the Renaissance despite the lapse of centuries; although we cannot accept this carnal and tormented by-product of ancient naturalism as a fully legitimate expression of human art, we are compelled to take note of the titanesque dimensions of this art in its most expressive productions. As in the case of the sixteenth century artists—such as Michelangelo, Donatello, Cellini—the motivating force here is the sensual cult of the human body combined with a neo-pagan perspective,[16] thus with various abuses of intelligence and also with the Greco-Roman sense of grandeur; but a grandeur of man and not that of God.

ity, in Beethoven there is something like the rupture of a dam or an explosion; and this climate of cataclysm is precisely what people appreciate.

[15] In Beethoven and other Germans, the titanism of the distant Renaissance is combined with the thunder of ancient Germany, and this aside from the presence of a quasi-angelic dimension of Christian origin.

[16] There is a curious analogy between Michelangelo's Last Judgment and Rodin's Gate of Hell: in both cases, the sensual and tormented beauty of the bodies goes hand in hand with an atmosphere of damnation, instead of communicating the serenity of the celestial shores as do the naked and on occasion amorous divinities of India and the Far East. With Bourdelle and Maillol, the ancient naturalism is attenuated. Exact observation in art certainly has its rights, but needs the regulatory and as it were musical element of stylization; art has to remain a writing, but a legible one.

—·⁞·—

One of the determining causes of the blossoming of genius from the end of the eighteenth century onwards—but above all in the nineteenth century—was the impoverishment of the environment: whereas in earlier times, in the Middle Ages especially, the environment was at once religious and chivalrous, that is to say laden with colors and melodies, if one may so express it, the Age of Philosophy and above all the Revolution, took away from the world all supranatural poetry, all the vital space extending upwards; men were more and more condemned to a hopeless horizontality, "profanity", and pettiness. This is what explains in part, or in certain cases, the cries of protest, of suffering, and despair, and also of nostalgia and beauty. If Beethoven, or any other great creator in the realm of art, had lived in the epoch of Charlemagne or of Saint Louis, their genius might have remained more inward, they would have found satisfactions and consolations—and above all, planes of realization—more in conformity with what constitutes the reason for the existence of human life. In a word, they would have found their center; or they would have perfected the center they already possessed by rendering it supernatural. Deprived of a real world, of a world which has a meaning and allows one to engage in liberating pursuits, many geniuses create for themselves an intense inner world, but one which is exteriorized on account of the need to manifest themselves; a world composed of nostalgia and grandeur, but in the final analysis with no meaning or efficacy other than that of a confession.

Such was also the case with Nietzsche, a volcanic genius if ever there was one; here, too, there is passionate exteriorization of an inward fire, but in a manner that is both deviated and demented; we have in mind here, not the Nietzschian philosophy, which in its literal expression is without interest,[17] but his poetical work, whose most intense expression is in part his *Zarathustra*. What this book, highly uneven as it is, manifests above all is the violent reaction of an *a priori* profound soul against a mediocre and paralyzing cultural

[17] This philosophy could have been a warning cry against the peril of a flattening and bastardizing humanitarianism, thus mortal for mankind; in point of fact, it was a combat against windmills and at the same time a seduction of the most perilous kind.

environment; Nietzsche's fault was to have only a sense of grandeur in the absence of all intellectual discernment. *Zarathustra* is basically the cry of a downtrodden grandeur, whence comes the heart-rending authenticity—the grandeur precisely—of certain passages; not all of them, certainly, and above all not those which express a half-Machiavellian, half-Darwinian philosophy, or literary cleverness. Be that as it may, Nietzsche's misfortune—like that of other men of genius, such as Napoleon—was to be born after the Renaissance and not before it; which indicates evidently an aspect of their nature, for nothing occurs by chance.

This was also Goethe's misfortune, a well-balanced and, from a certain standpoint, too well-balanced a genius. By this we mean to say that he was the victim of his epoch owing to the fact that humanism in general and Kantianism in particular had impaired his tendency towards a vast and finely-shaded wisdom; he thus became, quite paradoxically, the spokesman of a perfectly bourgeois "horizontality". His *Faust*, which starts off in the Middle Ages and in mystery, comes to an end, so to speak, in the nineteenth century and in philanthropy, leaving aside the final apotheosis which springs from the poet's Christian subconscious, without being able to compensate for the Kantian and Spinozan atmosphere of the work.[18] All the same, there is unquestionably great scope in the human substance of Goethe: a scope manifested by the at once lofty and generous quality of his mind;[19] and also, in a more intimate fashion, in those poems where he makes himself the "medium" of the popular soul, of medieval Germany all told; in so doing, he extends the spring-like and delicate lyricism of Walter von der Vogelweide, as if time had come to a stop.

A particularly problematical type of talent led astray from its true vocation is the novelist. Whereas in the Middle Ages novels still drew their inspiration from myths, legends, and religious and chivalrous

[18] The poet believes in the saving grace of an omnipresent divine Love, granted to whoever "strives unceasingly towards the good" ("*Wer immer strebend sich bemüht, den können wir erlösen*"); an eschatological optimism that combines in a strange fashion with eighteenth century deism on the one hand, and with esoteric knowledge of hermetic and cabalistic origin on the other hand; the incoherence is flagrant.

[19] We find the same traits in Schiller, with a slightly different accentuation; thus it is inadmissible that people should heap sarcasms on the moving idealism of this poet—as is fashionable nowadays in Germanic countries—for there was in him a truly authentic moral elevation and sense of grandeur, as is demonstrated especially by his ballads.

ideals, they became from a certain period onwards more and more profane,[20] even chatty and insignificant: their authors, instead of living their own lives, lived the lives of their imaginary personages one after the other. A Balzac, a Dickens, a Tolstoy, a Dostoevsky lived outside of themselves, giving their blood to phantoms, while inciting their readers to do the same: to waste their lives by burying themselves in the lives of others, with the aggravating circumstance that these others were neither heroes nor saints and, what is more, never existed. These remarks can apply to that whole universe of dreams termed "culture": flooded by literary opium, siren songs, vampirizing and—to say the least—useless productions, people live on the fringe of the natural world and its demands, and consequently on the fringe—or at the antipodes—of the "one thing needful". The nineteenth century—with its garrulous and irresponsible novelists, its "*poètes maudits*", its creators of poisonous operas, its unhappy artists, in short, with all of its useless idolatries and all of its blind alleys leading to despair—was bound to crash against a wall, the fruit of its own absurdity; thus the First World War[21] was for the "*belle époque*" what the sinking of the Titanic was for the elegant and decadent society that happened to be on board, or what Reading Gaol was for Oscar Wilde, analogically speaking.

Like other writers or artists, Wilde offers isolated values—we are thinking here of his tales[22]—which one would like to see in another

[20] Cervantes is in certain respects an exception—and certainly not the only one—in that his work serves as the vehicle for elements of philosophy and of symbolism, making one think of Shakespeare. As a literary genre, the theater is much less problematical than the novel, if only on account of its more disciplined and less time-consuming character. Calderón's plays prolong—in different degrees—the "mysteries" of the Middle Ages and exercise a didactic and spiritual function, in the manner of the tragedies of Antiquity, which were intended to provoke a catharsis.

[21] Of which the Second World War was only a belated continuation and conclusion.

[22] The best tales belong to poetry rather than to novels; they are in a way prose poems, inspired by the traditional models of popular tales containing an initiatory intention. We may note that Andersen does not have Wilde's capacity, but has the merit of having the soul of a child.

general context but of which it may be said, at least, that beauty always transmits a celestial dew-drop, if only for an instant. Divining in him a mystical dimension—his cult of beauty was only its golden shadow—one pities the author and one would like to save him from his morbid and futile side;[23] one may in any case suppose that his conversion *in extremis*—after so many cruel trials—was an encounter with Mercy. We can have the same sentiment in several analogous cases, where regret and hope prevail over a feeling of uneasiness, or even irritation.

Among the classic cases of self-destructive individualism we may mention the poet Lenau—half-German, half-Hungarian—who personifies the drama of a pessimistic narcissism sinking into melancholy and insanity. Such destinies are almost inconceivable in a religious and traditional climate; as inconceivable as the general phenomenon of a culture claiming to be an end in itself. No doubt, sadness has its beauty; it evokes a nostalgia which takes us beyond ourselves by purifying us, and consequently it evokes distant shores far from the disappointing narrowness of our earthly dreams; as the lyricism of the *Vita Nuova* testifies. Sadness has a right to be related to the song of Orpheus, but not to that of the sirens.[24]

There are also unhappy painters, such as Van Gogh and Gauguin, who are bearers of certain incontestable values—otherwise there would be no point in speaking about them; here too, the qualities are partial in the sense that the lack of discernment and spirituality makes itself felt—at least in certain figures—despite the prestige of the style.[25] But what counts here is not so much the value of this or

[23] Or save him from himself, since he personifies the tragic trajectory—or the total cycle—of quasi-divinized pleasure: of ultra-refined and intellectualized hedonism wishing to live itself out, down to its ineluctable ontological consequences. As soon as enjoyment is taken for an end in itself, and in the absence of a vertical and spiritual dimension which, by supernaturalizing it, would lend it the permanence of the archetypes, it presses on fatally towards the suicide it bears within itself. In saying in his "Ballad" that "each man kills the thing he loves", the poet expresses the intrinsic tragedy, not of love, but of pleasure become idol.

[24] Thus Saint Francis of Sales, who was certainly not lacking in sensibility, could say that "a sad saint is a sorry sort of saint"; he has in mind here a melancholy which erodes the theological virtues, precisely. Krishna's flute is the very image of ascending, not descending, nostalgia; sweetness of salvation, not of perdition.

[25] One should not forget—but the modernists will never admit it—that the choice of the subject matter is a part of art, and that the subject, far from being the "anecdote" of the work, as some people stupidly assert, is on the contrary its reason for being.

that pictorial style, as the drama—typical for the modern West—of normally intelligent men who sell their souls to a creative activity which no one asks of them and of which no one has any need, they themselves no more than others; who make a religion of their profane and individualistic art and who, so to speak, die martyrs for a cause not worth the trouble.

We meet in all arts with a type of genius which, like a display of fireworks, burns itself out in a single significant work, or in two or three works born of a single burst of inspiration. This is the case with Bizet, a medium—if one may say so—of the Hispano-Provençal soul, or more particularly of the passionate and at the same time tragic romanticism of bull fighting; with accentuations which, in the last analysis, go back to heroic chivalry and to the lyricism of the troubadours; of this, however, the great majority of his listeners are scarcely aware.

To come back to literature and to its least attractive aspects: an Ibsen and a Strindberg are the very types of talent wishing to make itself the spokesman of a thesis that is excessive, revolutionary, subversive, and in the highest degree individualistic and anarchic; in the nineteenth century, to be original at this price was like a mark of distinction—"after me the flood". This kind of talent—or of genius, as the case may be—makes one think of children who play with fire, or of Goethe's sorcerer's apprentice: these people play with everything, with religion, with the social order, with mental equilibrium, provided they can safeguard their originality; an originality which, retrospectively, reveals itself to be a perfect banality, because nothing is more banal than fashion, no matter how ostentatiously strident.

This calls for a general remark here, which has nothing to do with the considerations immediately above: our intention is not—and cannot be—to present a survey of art and literature, so there is no point in asking why we do not mention this or that particularly prominent genius. A Victor Hugo, for example; if we have not spoken of this sumptuous and long-winded spokesman of French romanticism, it is because neither his personality nor his destiny could merit a substantial commentary on our part; and the same remark applies to

As a matter of fact, the subjects of portraitists are all too often lacking in interest and consequently have nothing to communicate; the landscapists are fortunate in that they avoid this pitfall.

every other typologically equivalent celebrity. We shall not say anything very noteworthy therefore in pointing out that the author of the *Orientales*—like so many other creators of art—lives only through his productions, and that he puffs himself up and finally becomes hardened in the passionate projection of himself; and he does all this while enclosing his readers in an intense and despairing horizontality while inculcating in them a false idea of human grandeur, or of grandeur as such. As a result, humanism—in becoming humanitarianism—entails equally a false idea of human misery, the full eschatological dimension of which people take great care not to perceive; this humanism, furthermore, is quite likely to end in demagogy. And one knows from experience that, amongst the standard-bearers of integral humanism, megalomaniacal idealism gets along well with moral pettiness—on the political plane notably.

Be that as it may, this fragile and almost dreamlike world of totally profane genius and "culture" lasted barely two centuries; born more or less in the middle of the eighteenth century, it died about the middle of the twentieth century, after offering a burst of fireworks in the course of the previous century—the century that believed itself to be eternal. The protagonists die and the audience along with them; and the protagonists with the audience.

No doubt it will be objected that the flux of culture continues, since there are always new writers and new artists, whatever may be their worth or lack thereof; this is true, but it is no longer the same culture; living as it does on forgetfulness, it is no longer the culture which, on the contrary, once lived on remembrance.

—— ·:· ——

A particularly problematical sector of a culture set against a humanist background is philosophical production, where naive pretension and impious ambition intrude into the affairs of universal Truth, which is a very serious problem; the desire for originality on this plane is one of the least pardonable of sins. That said, and apart from the fact that one should not confuse cleverness with intelligence, one will note that there is intelligence everywhere, and therefore it is a truism to assert that the least of philosophers can sometimes say things which make sense. But, irrespective of this aspect of the question, it is paradoxical to say the least that those who are readily considered as being "thinkers" are not always those who know how to think—far from it—and that there are men who feel they have a vocation to think precisely because they are unable to evaluate all that this function implies.

As for doctrines—and this is an entirely different viewpoint—one has to recognize that profane philosophy benefits sometimes, and even fairly often in certain respects, from extenuating circumstances given the fact that the inadequacies of contemporary theology and confessional discord provoke with good reason doubts and reactions; thus philosophers are more or less victims, at least inasmuch as they are sincere. For the truths of the *philosophia perennis*, largely disregarded by average theologians, require something in the human intelligence to take their place; this explains, not the whole phenomenon of modern thought of course, but its most respectable or more excusable aspects.[26] But there is also, over and above the vain fluctuations of specifically profane thought, the spiritualist renewal of a Maine de Biran—whose merits we cannot overlook—not to mention the prolongations of ancient theosophy in the case of a Saint-Martin and a Baader, and partially in a Schelling.

Coming back now to the flood of philosophical literature—and it is indeed to this flood that the Hegelian dialectic could be applied—the most serious reproach we can make concerning the general run of these "thinkers" is their lack of intuition of the real and consequently their lack of sense of proportions; or the short-sightedness and disrespectful casualness with which they handle the weightiest questions human intelligence can conceive of, and to which centuries or even millennia of spiritual consciousness have provided the answer.

And while we are in this context, perhaps it is worthwhile to mention a phenomenon as uncalled for as it is irritating, that of the philosopher, or so-called philosopher, who imagines he can support his aberrant theses by means of novels and plays, because this comes down to inventing cock-and-bull stories in order to prove that two and two make five; this phenomenon is all too typical of a mentality

[26] Leaving aside the instances of culpable negligence—such as is the case of liberal theologians for example—not everyone feels obliged to plunge into the twists and turns of Scholasticism, all the more so since it is not accepted by the Eastern Orthodox Church which is, after all, strictly traditional, nor by the Protestants intent on adhering to Scripture.

that does not see the absurdity of intelligence denying intelligence. It is as if one were to paraphrase Descartes' *cogito ergo sum* upside down, postulating in fact that "I am; therefore I do not think."

Normally, the vocation of a thinker is synonymous with the sense of responsibility. The art of thinking is not the same thing as the joy of life; he who wishes to know how to think, must know how to die.

There is a side of "bourgeois culture" which reveals all its pettiness, and that is its aspect of conventional routine, its lack of imagination, in short its unconsciousness and its vanity: not for an instant is it asked, "What is the good of all this?"; there is not one author who asks whether it is worthwhile writing a new story after an untold number of other stories; it would seem as though they wrote them simply because others have done so, and because they do not see why one should not do so and why one should not gain the glory that others have gained.[27] It is a *perpetuum mobile* nothing can stop, except a catastrophe or, less tragically, the progressive disappearance of readers; there is no celebrity without an audience, as we have said earlier.[28] And this is what has happened to some extent: past authors whose prestige seemed assured are no longer read; the general public has other needs, other resources, and other distractions, however base they may be. More and more, culture becomes the absence of culture: the senseless habit of cutting oneself off from one's roots and of forgetting where one comes from.

One of the subjective reasons for what we may call "cultural routine" is that man does not like to face perdition alone, as a consequence he likes to find accomplices for a perdition in common; this is what profane culture does, consciously or unconsciously, but not innocently, because man bears deep within himself the instinct of his

[27] "To be famous and to be loved", as Balzac said.

[28] Much as Léon Bloy clung to the lifelines of religion, his imagination was nonetheless confined to the closed universe of literature, and it was a waste of time for him to fulminate against his colleagues and his accomplices. In too many cases, religious belief has strangely little power over the imagination, and this is still another effect of immanent humanism.

reason for being and of his vocation. The Oriental civilizations have often been reproached for their cultural sterility, that is to say for the fact that they do not comprise a continuous stream of literary, artistic, and philosophical production; we believe that we can be dispensed at this point from having to explain the reasons for this.

Even more detestable than unimaginative "conventionalism" is the obsession with change along with the repetitious infidelities it implies: it is the need to "burn what one has worshipped" and, on occasion, to "worship what one has burned".[29] Classicism, romanticism, realism, naturalism, symbolism, psychological novels, social novels, and so on and so forth; and strangest of all is that one ceases at each new stage to understand what previously one had understood perfectly; or one pretends not to understand it any longer, for fear of being left behind. One has no choice but to remember Racine and Corneille—above all Molière who, as everyone knows, is still comically entertaining—or Pascal,[30] in the context of "culture" precisely; one is also obliged to accept La Fontaine and Perrault for the sake of children. But few are those who still know and appreciate a Louise Labé, whose sonnets are in no way inferior to those either of Petrarch, Michelangelo, or Shakespeare; otherwise a poet as refined as Rilke would not have taken the trouble to translate them and in so doing turn them into new masterpieces.

No doubt, a man can grow weary of something he has busied himself with too much, or with which he has busied himself too superficially; but it does not follow from this that he has a right to despise it, especially if there is nothing in it warranting either weariness or contempt. Weariness itself can be the sign of a warped mentality, and the tendency to arbitrary mockery certainly is so; quite simply, if we have had enough of something, whether rightly or wrongly, all we have to do is to busy ourselves with something else; there is no reason why we should speak disparagingly of it; he who has studied Aristotle too much can go and play the violin. But it is a fact—as Schiller has said—that "the world likes to blacken whatever shines, and drag the sublime into the dust. . .".

[29] This is exactly what the Renaissance did in "burning" the symbolist Middle Ages and in "worshipping" naturalistic Antiquity.

[30] To also mention a philosopher, the "most valid" one that France has known since the Middle Ages.

—·:·—

Whereas the traditional literatures and arts manifest all their modes and all their diversity in a simultaneous manner—with, however, differences of accentuation depending on the epochs—the West, starting with the Renaissance, manifests its cultural modes in a successive manner, following a route bristling with anathematizations and glorifications. The reason for this is in the last analysis a profound ethnic heterogeneity: that is to say, a certain incompatibility, among Europeans, between the Aryan and Semitic minds on the one hand, and between the Roman and Germanic mentalities on the other; it is a situation in a certain sense equivalent to what the Hindus call a "mixture of castes", with the difference that the constituent elements are not hierarchized, but simply disparate—the West being in addition more individualistic than the East.

A characteristic trait of Western culture from the late Middle Ages onwards is, moreover, a certain feminization: indeed, the masculine costume manifests outwardly, at least in the upper classes and above all among the princes, an excessive need to please women, which is a telling sign; whereas in the culture in general, we can observe an increase in the imaginative and emotive sensibility, in short an expressivity which strictly speaking goes too far and renders souls worldly instead of interiorizing them. The distant cause of this trait could be in part the respect which, according to Tacitus, the Germans had for woman—a respect we are far from blaming—but this quite normal and praiseworthy feature would have been without any problematical consequences if there had not been another much more determinative factor, namely the Christian scission of society into clerics and laymen; because of this, lay society grew into a separate humanity which came more and more to believe that it had a right to worldliness, wherein woman—whether she liked it or not—evidently played a leading role.[31] We mention this aspect of Western culture because it explains

[31] A sign of this lay autocracy and the worldliness resulting from it is, as regards vestimentary manifestations, the low-cut neckline of women, already criticized by Dante and paradoxical not only from the standpoint of Christian asceticism, but also from the standpoint of Semitic legalism which, precisely, makes no distinction between clerics and laymen since it attributes a sacred character to society as a whole. It is not the phenomenon of uncovering the flesh which is astonishing here—for it exists

a certain exteriorized and hypersensitive style of genius; and let us not forget to add that all this pertains to the mystery of Eve, and not to that of Mary which pertains to ascending *Māyā*.

One has to react against the prejudice that every man of genius, even the most eminent intellectual, is necessarily intelligent, and that it is enough for an Einstein to be intelligent in mathematics for him to be equally intelligent in other domains—in politics for example—which in fact was certainly not the case. There are men who are geniuses in a single domain and who are all the less gifted in other respects; examples of fragmentary, unilateral, asymmetric, disproportional genius are provided above all by those writers or artists—and they are numerous—who compensate for their creative sublimity by a trivial or even odious character. In a normal world, one could readily do without their creations and the hidden poison they contain and transmit in most cases; not in all cases though, since there is the possibility of intermittent "mediumship", as we have explained above.

Among many men of varying genius we can see a "brilliant intelligence" having no connection either with metaphysical truth or with eschatological reality; now the definition of integral or essential, and thus efficacious, intelligence is adequation to the real, both "horizontal" and "vertical", terrestrial and celestial. A consciousness having neither the sense of priorities nor that of proportions is not really intelligence; it is at the very most a reflection of intelligence in the mirror of the mind, and we are quite willing to have it called "intelligence" in an entirely relative and provisional sense; human discernment may be exercised in a very limited field, but the mental activity involved is still discernment. Conversely, it can happen that a spiritually—thus

legitimately in Hinduism and elsewhere—but the fact that this phenomenon occurs in a Christian setting; the same remark holds good for the prominence of the male organs in certain costumes of the late Middle Ages. It could also be said that the frivolous character of lay customs—notably the balls—serves as the counterpart for the exaggerated rigorism of the convents, and that this far too ostentatious disparity points to a disequilibrium which is the fomenter of all sorts of subsequent oscillations. In India, the maharajah covered with pearls and the *yogin* covered with ashes are certainly dissimilar, but both are "divine images".

fundamentally—intelligent man lacks intelligence practically speaking on the plane of earthly things or some of them; but that is because, rightly or wrongly, he cannot bring himself to take an interest in them.[32]

To come back to the poets: it is impossible to deny that the plays of Montherlant are quite intelligent in their way, but the fact that the author—who possessed an excessively uneven and contradictory character[33]—scarcely manifested any discernment outside of dramatic art, illustrates well enough the relativity and the precariousness of what we may call "worldly intelligence". One should not forget in this context the role of passions: pride limits intelligence, which amounts to saying that in the last analysis it slays it: it destroys its essential functions, while possibly allowing the surface mechanism to remain, as if in mockery.[34]

In this order of ideas—and leaving aside the question of pride—we might also express ourselves as follows: in a certain sense it was very intelligent on the part of the Greeks and their emulators to have represented the human body in all its exactness and all its contingency; but more fundamentally, it was quite unintelligent on their part to have taken this trouble and to have neglected other modes of adequation, those precisely which were developed by the Hindus and the Buddhists. Intelligence as such is above all the sense of priorities and proportions, as we have pointed out above; it implies *a priori* a sense of the Absolute and of the hierarchy of corresponding values.

[32] It is no exaggeration on our part to say that for some people the most intelligent men are the Nobel prize winners in physics; given such blunders, it is quite excusable to say things which run the risk of being truisms.

[33] That is to say that the plebeian side of his personality was opposed to the aristocratic side, just as in Heine the cynical was opposed to the lyrical; in both cases, the trouble is not in the bipolarity but in the antagonism between the two poles.

[34] The meaning of human life is sanctification, without which man would not be man. "Life is no longer worthy of me", said—or thought he could say—an individualist who refused to accept a trial; whereas every man ought to say from the outset "I am not worthy of life", while accepting the trial in order to become worthy of it. Because, for man to be worthy of life is to be worthy of God; without forgetting that *Domine non sum dignus*, which expresses another relationship.

Thus, neither efficacy in a particular domain nor the phenomenon of genius are necessarily identified with intelligence as such. Another error of evaluation to be refuted is the odd habit of seeing genius where there is none; this is to confuse genius with extravagance, snobbery, cynicism, and brazen boldness, and it is to seek an object of worship because one no longer has God. Or again, it is to worship oneself in an artificial and illusory projection; or it is quite simply to adulate vice and darkness.

Nothing is easier than to be original using a false absolute, all the more so when this absolute is negative, for it is easier to destroy than to build. Humanism is the reign of horizontality, either naive or perfidious; and since it is also—and by that very fact—the negation of the Absolute, it is an open door to a multitude of sham absolutes, which in addition are often negative, subversive, and destructive. It is not too difficult to be original with such intentions and such means; it is enough for someone to stumble onto the idea. It should be noted that subversion includes not only philosophical and moral schemes designed to undermine the normal order of things, but also—in literature and on a seemingly harmless plane—all that can satisfy an unhealthy curiosity: namely all the stories that are bizarrely fantastic, grotesque, lugubrious, "dark", thus satanic in their way, and made to predispose men to all kinds of excesses and perversions; this is the sinister side of romanticism. Having no qualms for being "childlike", nor the slightest concern for being "adult", we are quite happy to do without these somber lunacies, and are fully satisfied with Snow White and Sleeping Beauty.

Literary "realism" is properly subversive because it aims at reducing reality to the vilest contingencies of nature or chance, instead of leading it back to its archetypes and thus to the divine intentions, in short, to the essential which any normal man should perceive without difficulty, and which any man perceives in love notably, or with respect to any phenomenon that gives rise to admiration. This is, moreover, the mission of art: to remove the shells in order to reveal the kernels; to distill the materials until the essences are extracted. Nobleness is nothing if not a natural predisposition for this alchemy, and of this on all planes.

As for subversion, on the plane of ideologies there are not only those which are frankly pernicious, thus negative despite their masks, there are also those which are formally positive—more or less—but limitative and poisonous and ultimately destructive in their way: such as nationalism and other narcissistic fanaticisms; the majority—if not all—are as ephemeral as they are shortsighted. And the worst among these false idealisms are, in certain respects, those that annex and adulterate religion.

But let us come back to the question of originality which we broached above. In order to define true originality, we shall say this: art in the broadest sense is the crystallization of archetypal values, and not a mere copy of the phenomena of nature or of the soul *tale quale*; and this is why the terms "reality" and "realism" have another meaning in art than in the sciences; the latter record phenomena without disregarding accidental and insignificant contingencies, whereas art, on the contrary—as we have said—works to remove shells in order to extract gold from "dense matter". Positive originality could never arise from our desire; it proceeds from the combination of our traditional environment and our legitimate personality, a combination sown with the archetypes likely to manifest themselves in it, and inclined to do so. In a word, art is the quest for—and the revelation of—the center, within us as well as around us.

At the opposite extreme of the false genius people glorify is situated the true genius which people ignore: among famous men, Lincoln is one such example, he who owes a large part of his popularity to the fact that people took him—and still take him—for the incarnation of the average American, one as average as possible. This he absolutely was not, and could not have been, precisely because he was a man of genius, a man whose intelligence, capacity—and also nobility of character—went far beyond the level of the average person.[35]

[35] It was during Lincoln's administration that the formula "In God we trust" was first introduced in coinage, and it was Lincoln who made Thanksgiving Day a national holiday. We should like to mention in this context the greatness of soul of another statesman, Chiang Kai-shek: at the end of the Second World War he made a declaration enjoining his countrymen not to hate the Japanese people, which was a gesture of exceptional lucidity and courage; not in itself, because there is no such thing as a people deserving hatred, but given human nature as well as the circumstances.

Another case—and a rather peculiar one—of a genius in full possession of his center is Gandhi; a peculiar case, we say, because he seems to be a borderline possibility from the standpoint of sanctity. Technically speaking, Gandhi can no doubt be included in the category of saints; but from a traditional viewpoint, the question remains open. Against him, there are his somewhat too liberal, even Tolstoian ideas, although—despite certain reservations—he rejected neither the Vedas nor the castes; in his favor, one can mention his practice of *japa-yoga*, which is a good argument as far as "traditionality" is concerned, but not of sanctity as such. We take note of the phenomenon here but without wishing to settle the question in a peremptory manner; what we have here is a possibility that is characteristic of the cyclical period in which we live: a period of ambiguities, paradoxes, and also of exceptions. Given the fact that Gandhi did not found anything and that he had no disciples in the strict sense of the term, the question of his degree of spirituality can, we repeat, be left unanswered.[36]

The question of normal genius, not conditioned by some cultural abuse, allows us to move on to the following considerations, which have their importance in this context. The racist argument that the whites, and among them the Europeans, have more genius than other races obviously loses much of its value—to say the least—in the light of what we have said about humanism and its consequences; because how could one fail to see that neither a hypertrophy nor a deviation can constitute an intrinsic superiority? Nonetheless, when considering genius under its natural and legitimate aspect, one has a right to ask whether this phenomenon is also encountered among non-literate peoples, given the fact that they do not seem to provide any such examples; we reply without hesitation that genius lies within human nature and that it must be possible for it to occur wherever there are men. Obviously, the manifestation of genius depends on such cultural materials as are at the disposal of a racial or ethnic group; since these materials are relatively meager among the peoples in question, the manifestations of genius must be all the more intangible and easily forgotten, except for legends and proverbial expressions.[37]

[36] But we must insist emphatically on the factor that we have just pointed out, namely that Gandhi did not exercise the function of a spiritual master; our "tolerance" thus cannot be taken as opening the door to any technical deviation from the rule.

[37] "Not every man is the son of Gaika", the Zulus say, evoking the memory of a particularly gifted and glorious chief, but who has disappeared in the mists of time.

Non-literate ethnic groups have at their disposal three ways of manifesting genius, in keeping with their way of life: firstly the martial and royal genius; secondly, the oratorical and epic genius;[38] and thirdly, the contemplative genius, but this one rarely leaves any traces, whereas the two preceding types leave them more easily, the second one especially. If these ethnic groups have no sense of history, it is for the same reason that they have no writing: their entire conception of life is so to speak rooted in an "eternal present" and in a flux of things wherein the individual counts for nothing; time being a spiroidal movement around an invisible and immutable Center.

A factor which should not be overlooked when one is surprised at the lack of "culture" among non-literate peoples is that the nature surrounding them furnishes all the nourishment that the soul requires; these ethnic groups feel no need to superimpose on the riches and beauties of nature riches and beauties springing from the imagination and creativity of men; they feel no need to listen to human language rather than to the language of the Great Spirit.[39] On the one hand, the lack of urban culture can assuredly be the result of degeneration; but on the other hand, this lack can be explained by a particular perspective and a free choice; both causes can evidently be combined. It should not be overlooked that the Hindu *sannyāsin*, who lives in the forest, does not worry about "culture", any more than does a Christian hermit; this is not an absolute criterion, but it nonetheless has its importance.

[38] There have been true Demosthenes among the orators of the American Indians. Some of their speeches, either complete or in fragments thereof, have been preserved in writing; the upright, generous, and moving grandeur of their language is quite striking. We may mention here, by way of examples, three men of genius belonging to the red race: first, Hinmaton-Yalatkit ("Chief Joseph"), chief of the Sahaptin (Nez Percés), who in the opinion of American army officers was a prodigious strategist; then the Shawnee chief Tecumseh, who lived some decades earlier—at the beginning of the nineteenth century—and whose qualities as a statesman and magnanimous hero are almost proverbial in the New World; and finally Tammany or Tamanend, a sachem of the Leni-Lenape (Delawares)—in the seventeenth century—who enjoyed a reputation for wisdom and holiness not only among the Indians, but even among the whites, who went as far as venerating him as the "patron of America" and gave his name to several of their societies.

[39] The remark of a Sioux chief after a visit to a museum of fine arts: "You whites are strange men; you destroy the beauties of nature, then you daub a board with colors and call it a masterpiece."

And one has to keep clearly in mind the following: the marvels of the basilicas and the cathedrals, of the iconostases and the altar pieces, as well as the splendors of Buddhist Tibeto-Mongol and Japanese art or, prior to it, those of Hindu art, not forgetting the summits of the corresponding literatures—all this did not exist in the primitive epochs of these various traditions, epochs which were precisely the "golden ages" of these spiritual universes. Thus the marvels of traditional culture seem like the swan songs of the celestial messages: in other words, to the extent that the message runs the risk of being lost, or is effectively lost, a need is felt—and Heaven itself feels this need—to exteriorize gloriously all that men are no longer capable of perceiving within themselves. Thenceforth it was outward things that had to remind men where their center lies; it is true that this is in principle the role of virgin nature, but in fact its language is only grasped where it takes on traditionally the function of a sanctuary.[40] Moreover, the two perspectives—sacred art and virgin nature—are not mutually exclusive, as is shown notably by Zen Buddhism; this proves that neither can altogether replace the other.

All that we have said above concerning non-literate peoples does not mean that they have no culture in the fully legitimate sense. Integrally human culture is linked to participation in the sacred, and this obviously has no indispensable connection with literacy or with sedentary civilization. The immense stores of oral tradition and diverse forms of artistic expression testify to a formerly prodigious richness of soul in ancient man, and this was originally linked to sacred wisdom, of which virgin nature, precisely, is the primordial expression—an expression transparent to the integral symbolist mentality, although scarcely so to modern "culturism".

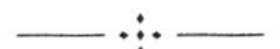

After having spoken at the beginning of this account of the hierarchical types of mankind—namely of the "intrinsic" and not simply institutional castes—we then engaged in reflections about an entirely

[40] Among the ancient Aryans, from India to Ireland—except, more or less, the Mediterraneans in historic times—and in our day still among the shamanist peoples, Asiatic and American.

different subject, that of genius, with digressions and illustrations for which we see no reason to apologize. In both cases, that of genius as well as that of the castes, it is always a question of man and his center: either because nature has bestowed on man a given personal center and consequently a particular fundamental tendency and a particular conception of duty and happiness—this is precisely what "caste" is—or because man, whatever his basis or starting point may be, embarks on the search for his center and his reason for being.

To speak of humanism is to speak of individualism, and to speak of individualism it to speak of narcissism and, as a result, of a breaching of that protective wall which is the human norm; thus of a rupture of equilibrium between the subjective and the objective, or between wandering sensibility and pure intelligence. However, it is not easy to have completely unmixed feelings on the subject of profane "cultural" genius: if, on the one hand, one must condemn humanism and the literary and artistic principles derived from it, one cannot, on the other hand, help recognizing the value of this or that archetypal inspiration, and possibly the personal qualities of a particular author; hence one can hardly escape a certain ambiguity. And the fact that a work of art, by reason of its cosmic message, can transmit values graspable only by a few—just as wine can at the same time do good to some and harm to others—this fact makes our judgments in many cases, if not objectively less precise, at least subjectively more hesitant; although it is always possible to simplify the problem by specifying in what respect a given work has value.

Be that as it may, what we wish to suggest in most of our considerations on modern genius is that humanistic culture, insofar as it functions as an ideology and therefore as a religion, consists essentially in ignoring three things: firstly, what God is, because it does not accord primacy to Him; secondly, what man is, because it puts him in the place of God; thirdly, what the meaning of life is, because this culture limits itself to playing with evanescent things and to plunging into them with criminal unconsciousness. In a word, there is nothing more inhuman than humanism, by the fact that it, so to speak, decapitates man: in wishing to make of him an animal which is perfect, it succeeds in turning him into a perfect animal; not all at once—because it has the fragmentary merit of abolishing certain barbaric traits—but in the long run, since it inevitably ends by "re-barbarizing" society, while "dehumanizing" it *ipso facto* in depth. A fragmentary merit, we say, because the softening of customs is good only on condition that it not corrupt man, that it not unleash criminality, nor open the door to all possible perversions. In the nineteenth century it was still possible to believe in an indefinite moral progress; in the twentieth century came the brutal awakening; people were forced to recognize that one cannot improve man by finding contentment on the surface while destroying the foundations.

Thus, there is no doubt that talent or genius does not constitute a value in itself. One thing is absolutely certain—so much so that one hesitates to mention it—and that is that the best way to have genius is to have it through wisdom and virtue, hence through holiness. Creative genius can certainly be added to this plenitude as a supplementary gift—for others even more than for the one who possesses it—with the mission of transmitting elements of interiorization and thereby of liberation. Clearly, pure spirituality suffices unto itself; but no one will reproach Dante for having known how to write, nor Fra Angelico for having known how to paint.

To return to the first subject of our account: whatever the fundamental differences may be between the hierarchized human types—from the standpoint of that central core that constitutes the substance of a person—there is what we may call, not without reservations of course, "religious egalitarianism", to which we have alluded before; man before the face of God is always man and nothing else, whether he possesses a valid center or lacks one. And man, being what he is, is always free to choose his center, his identity, and his destiny, to build his house either on sand or on a rock.

"Free to choose": but in reality, the man who is conscious of his interest and concerned with his happiness has no choice; the purpose of freedom is to enable us to choose what we are in the depths of our heart. We are intrinsically free to the extent that we have a center which frees us: a center which, far from confining us, dilates us by offering us an inward space without limits and without shadows; and this center is in the last analysis the only one there is.

2. Overview of Anthropology

When we speak of man, what we have in mind first of all is human nature as such, that is, inasmuch as it is distinguished from animal nature. Specifically human nature is made of centrality and totality, and hence of objectivity; objectivity being the capacity to step outside oneself, while centrality and totality are the capacity to conceive the Absolute. Firstly, objectivity of intelligence: the capacity to see things as they are in themselves; next, objectivity of will, hence free will; and finally, objectivity of sentiment, or of soul if one prefers: the capacity for charity, disinterested love, compassion. "*Noblesse oblige*": the "human miracle" must have a reason for being that is proportioned to its nature, and this is what predestines—or "condemns"—man to surpass himself; man is totally himself only by transcending himself. Quite paradoxically, it is only in transcending himself that man reaches his proper level; and no less paradoxically, by refusing to transcend himself he sinks below the animals which—by their form and mode of passive contemplativity—partake adequately and innocently in a celestial archetype; in a certain respect, a noble animal is superior to a vile man.

The individual worth of a man may be either physical, psychic, or intellectual, or a combination of these. The most outward values are beauty and bodily health; the first manifests our "deiformity", and the second is added to it as a norm. Next there is moral value, which is beauty of soul that partakes also in intelligence; and finally there is the value of intelligence itself. Man is responsible neither for his beauty nor for his ugliness—except to some extent for the manner of his aging—but this does not prevent beauty as such from being a value which can contribute to spiritual alchemy; ugliness may also contribute to it, but in an indirect fashion and *a contrario*, as a support for the realization of certain truths. As for soundness of character, man is clearly responsible for it; if he possesses it by nature, he must maintain it, for he can lose it; if he does not possess it, he must acquire it.

And man is so made that his intelligence has no effective value unless it be combined with a virtuous character. Besides, no virtuous man is altogether deprived of intelligence; while the intellectual capacity of an intelligent man has no value except through truth.

Intelligence and virtue are in conformity with their reason for being only through their supernatural contents or archetypes; in a word, man is not fully human unless he transcends himself, hence, first of all through self-domination.

In what follows, we shall have to mention facts which are no doubt all too evident, but our subject obliges us to do so, for no aspect of man can be left unmentioned, even the most outward. Thus our exposition will by the nature of things resemble an enumeration rather than a speculation, at least in part, and in any case truisms have their role to play in introducing a subject. Therefore, if our exposition seems somewhat heterogeneous, the reason for this lies in our subject itself, in the complexity of the human phenomenon; we wish to be conscientious without having to be too pedantic.

If on the one hand every man possesses a body, a soul, and a spirit, on the other hand men are differentiated by gender and age. Gender—whether masculine or feminine—must be considered from the following three standpoints: first, the standpoint of sexuality properly so called, which is the plane of physiological, psychological, functional, and social inequality—but also of complementarity; then, the standpoint of their common humanity—each sex being human and not something else—and this is the plane of equality and friendship; in this connection, a woman may be superior to a man, precisely because she is human and not merely feminine; nonetheless, feminine nature excludes, if not the summits of spirituality, then at least certain functions that are in fact more or less social. The third standpoint to be considered is that of spiritual breadth: on this so to speak "tantric" plane, each sex assumes an almost divine role for the other; this is the domain of love, not only on the natural level, of course, but also and even more so on the supernatural and "alchemical" level.

Having spoken of sex, we must say something about age, even though the common experience of men in this sector furnishes all the necessary insights. Nonetheless, for the sake of completeness, we shall recall that childhood is the period of formation and learning; maturity, the period of actual and effective realization; late middle age, the period of consolidation, reparation, and the directing of others; and old age, the period of detachment and transcendence. Morning, day, afternoon, and night; or spring, summer, autumn, and winter. It could also be said that childhood is the paradise of innocence, youth the time of passions, maturity the time of work, and old age that of sadness; for it is far from being the case that old age is always the haven of wisdom; it is so in spiritually superior men or, more generally, in surroundings still imbued with real piety, but not in a humanistic, "horizontal", and more or less atheistic world, where the tendency of the old people is to try to seem young at all costs and to forget conspicuously the "one thing needful". Such an anomaly is scarcely found among traditional peoples or, for that matter, among barbaric peoples who, in more than one respect, are more normal than the ultra-civilized.

From the physiological point of view, age coincides with a degeneration; from the spiritual point of view the opposite takes place: age is an ascent towards another world.

On another differentiating plane, but purely psychological this time, is situated what the Hindus term "color" (*varna*), namely caste. These are the four fundamental tendencies of mankind,[1] and their corresponding aptitudes; tendencies and aptitudes of an essentially uneven worth, as is seen precisely in the Hindu system of castes, or as is seen in analogous systems in other civilizations, that of ancient Egypt for example, or that of the Far East. Nor should it be overlooked that the social hierarchy in Europe—the nobility, the clergy, and the bourgeoisie or "third estate"—unquestionably constituted castes, the nobility in particular; executioners, acrobats, prostitutes, and others were considered pariahs, rightly or wrongly as the case may be. But it is not of institutionalized—hence necessarily approximate—castes that we wish to speak here, but of natural castes, those based on the intrinsic nature of individuals; the institutional castes are merely their legal applications, and in fact they are more often symbolical rather than effective as regards the real potentialities of persons, above all in

[1] Not the "human race", as is often said; this expression is altogether inappropriate, for a species is not a race.

later times; nonetheless they have a certain practical and psychological justification, otherwise they would not exist traditionally.

The essential point here is that mankind is psychologically differentiated by gifts and by ideals: there is the ideal of the sage or the saint, then the ideal of the hero; next the ideal of the respectable and "reasonable" average man, and finally that of the man who seeks no more than the pleasures of the moment, and whose virtue consists in obeying and in being faithful. But, outside of men who are psychologically homogeneous, there is also the man "without a center", who is capable of "all and nothing", and who is readily an imitator and also a destroyer. Let us hasten to add, however, that in this world there are distinctions and shades of difference in everything, and that if we must take note of inferior human possibilities it is not in order to pronounce verdicts upon individuals; for "what is impossible for man, is possible for God."

We mentioned "gifts" above, and this allows us now to consider the phenomenon of talent or genius. First of all, it is all too clear that genius has value only through its content, and is even of no worth in the absence of human qualities which are incumbent on individuals; and that consequently, it would be better for a "great man" with a problematical character to have less talent and more virtue. The cause of genius is a hypertrophy or supersaturation due to heredity or, as the transmigrationists would say, to a certain *karma*, hence to the merits or demerits of a former life, as the case may be. The *karma* is in any case benefic when it is the vehicle of spiritual values or when it gives rise to them; obviously, the great sages and saints of all traditional climates were men of genius—but they were not merely that, precisely.

—— ·:· ——

On the plane of neutral factors—such as gender and age—one also has to distinguish human types: firstly racial and sub-racial, then "astrological", and finally strictly personal.

Since the same errors and confusions are always encountered on the subject of races, we think it worthwhile to make certain elementary points on the subject, even though they are in themselves of rather relative interest; but, all told, this is still part of our subject. Thus, there are three great racial types, the white, the yellow, and the black; then the more or less intermediate types, such as the black-white,[2] Malay, American Indian, and Polynesian races, as well as other groups of minimal importance. The three fundamental races represent—and cannot but represent—quasi-essential modes of mankind, and that is why each of the three racial types is encountered, in an attenuated and adapted manner, of course, within the other two races, with the psychological meaning each type comprises by its very form; this meaning could not be narrow, but on the contrary must be as vast and subtle as possible.

As regards the subsidiary races—not the intermediary races—we shall confine ourselves to enumerating those of the white race, namely, the "Nordics", the "Mediterraneans" and their brahmanical analogues in India, the "Dinarics" and their Armenoid or Assyroid analogues, the "Alpines"—one speaks improperly of a "Slavic" type—and the "Orientals"; and finally, the "Dravidians" of India and the northern Far East—also termed "Paleo-Asiatics"—to which are attached, perhaps, the Veddoid Australians, who are not of Melanesian stock. The reason for the existence of all the races and subsidiary races lies in the typological economy of humanity, otherwise they would not exist; man is differentiated by definition.[3]

What is important to recall here is that there is no Aryan, Semitic, Hamitic, or Uralo-Altaic race, nor a Germanic, Celtic, Latin, Slavic, or Greek race; even though there may be racial predominances in these linguistic groups, and even though each language corresponds to a greater or lesser extent to what may be called a "psychological race".

To return to the European subsidiary races—Nordic, Mediterranean, and others—nowhere do they coincide with peoples; all the

[2] Improperly termed "Hamitic" on account of the linguistic family of this name. In fact, certain tribes that are called "Hamitic" belong to the white race, others belong to the black race, the majority being more or less intermediary.

[3] To be concrete, we would say that Lincoln is a perfect example of the Dinaric type; and Washington, of the Nordic type. Napoleon furnishes us with the classical image of the Mediterranean type; Beethoven of the type termed Alpine. As for the Oriental type—this adjective having a specific meaning here —it is that of an Emir Abd el-Kader of Algeria or of a Ramakrishna; the superior Dravidian type being represented by a Ramana Maharshi. We should specify that the type termed "Oriental", brown in color, is found among all the eastern peoples of the white race, and even in Europe alongside the Mediterranean type; it is in the majority in Arabia, in the Iranian countries, and in North India.

European peoples include all the racial types enumerated above, with more or less strong predominances according to the region. And let us not forget to mention that to each racial or subsidiary racial type there corresponds a psychological type: the Nordic is distinguished by features different from those of the Mediterranean for example. But we may confine ourselves, on this plane, to the two following observations: firstly, there is no race or people possessing qualities only or defects only, and secondly, the individual is not necessarily limited by the average characteristics of the collectivity; as a human being he keeps in principle all of his freedom.

Here a remark is called for regarding individuals qualified as "typical" of a given racial group. The word "typical" has two altogether different meanings: on the one hand, it designates types which, in a given group, are particularly numerous—without necessarily representing the majority—while nevertheless exhibiting great differences among themselves; on the other hand, the same word designates types which may be small in number, but which are met with only within that group and nowhere else, even though there may always be exceptions to this rule. But it is an abuse to term the majority "typical" while refusing this attribute to the two categories just mentioned, for that would be a purely quantitative rather than qualitative point of view, and such an evaluation is contrary to the nature of things. From such a point of view, one could never consider as representative a type that embodies in the highest degree a racial, ethnic, and spiritual ideal—an archetype so to speak.

As for the question of physiognomy, there are not only types peculiar to the races, there are also what may be termed "astrological" types, which are found everywhere and which can coincide with given racial types; so much so that one cannot in every case determine whether a given type derives from a racial or astrological origin. One may well note, for example, that the Nordics are tall and dolichocephalic, yet there are necessarily pure Nordics who are small and brachycephalic, for the simple reason that the same typological possibilities are manifested in all the racial frameworks, independently of races and regional elaboration. This is precisely what certain racists are unaware of, or wish to be unaware of:[4] according to them, all the great

[4] Such as Chamberlain, Gobineau, Günther, and others. It is not the Scandinavians or the Germans who invented Nordic or Nordist racism; no race or people is responsible for it.

works of humanity are due to the Nordic race which, it would seem, is present everywhere; if they observe, in China for example, tall individuals with long faces, they claim that Vikings—or the ancestors of the Vikings—passed through there, and they explain all the achievements of Chinese civilization, above all the creation and expansion of the empire, by the presence of Nordic blood. They are unaware of the fact that in each race the repetition of certain types is due, not to mixtures, but to mankind's homogeneity and to the ubiquity of the same typological possibilities, not to mention the role of astrological types, the universality of the temperaments, and other factors both diversifying and repetitive.[5]

—— ·:· ——

Astrology teaches us that the sun, the moon, and the planets determine to a certain extent physical and psychic types in various ways, according to the signs of the zodiac in which they are situated. It is thus that one may distinguish Solar, Lunar, Mercurian, Venusian, Martian, Jupiterian, and Saturnian types, all of which comprise, as we have said, divergent modes, not to mention a host of intermediary or mixed types. We shall merely point out here that the Solar type has something active and radiant; the Lunar, something round, passive, and childlike; the Mercurian is light and elegant; the Venusian is gentle and charming; the Martian, square and aggressive; the Jupiterian, full and large, sometimes jovial; and the Saturnian, ascetic and morose.

But astral determinations are not everything, otherwise one could not explain how in a series of astrologically identical types with the same racial characteristics there are differences whose causes must pertain to an altogether different dimension; which comes down to asking why one person is not another. First of all there is the natural factor of heredity; next, the Hindus and Buddhists will put forth the argument of *karma*—actions and experiences situated in a former

[5] Both Don Quixote and Sancho Panza are—or could be—Mediterraneans; they represent a human opposition which, precisely because it is human, is found in all races. It would be ridiculous to claim that the "knight of the woeful countenance" is Dinaric because he is tall and bony, and that his squire is an Alpine because he is short and stocky.

life—although in certain respects, both these causes coincide. More fundamentally, we shall say that All-Possibility must manifest its potentialities on all planes, and that no determinism can limit the play of *Māyā*. The universe is woven not only of principles, but also of imponderables; mathematical qualities are joined to musical qualities. Finally, in human typology, one has also to take into account the degrees of spirituality and of non-spirituality, which are superimposed on the outward typological modalities, conferring upon them meanings—and modes of expressivity—of a new and strictly qualitative order.

The physical and psychic type of the individual, as we have said, is determined not only by astrological influences, but also by factors such as heredity and the law of *karma*; and this amounts to saying that all these factors are combined. The coincidence of the different determining factors is certainly not due to chance: it is explained by the total possibility the individual manifests, and which precisely determines this mysterious coincidence; this possibility is the first cause which governs the secondary causes, on the plane in question.

To observe that there are different human types and to be aware that their forms cannot be devoid of meaning, is to acknowledge that there is necessarily a science which studies this sector of anthropology. Fundamentally, this science—physiognomy—interprets three regions of the face: the forehead along with the eyes, then the nose, and then the mouth along with the chin; these elements correspond respectively to the intellective nature, the sensitive or "instinctive" nature, and the volitive nature. Moreover, as every form has a cause and a meaning, all the parts of the body are to some degree or other expressions of our being.[6]

But the individual is not ineluctably limited by his form, or his forms; he may be, but he may also not be; the form may be the expression of his substance, but it may also represent his *karma*—the effect of past actions or attitudes—in which case the individual is subject

[6] The hands, for example, which are the object of a particular science, chirology, from which chiromancy is derived.

to his form without necessarily being identified with it. The privative form will then manifest the past but not the person; a transitory accident but not the immortal substance; it is then a scar and not an open wound.[7] And this concerns the soul as well as the body: there are men who have become saints by becoming the opposite of what they were before; in reality, by finally becoming themselves.

—— ·:· ——

On the one hand, everything leads one to believe that it is major circumstances which create the individual; on the other hand, it is the individual possibility that determines the circumstances. It is the combination of the possibilities that weave that veil of *Māyā* which is the world; the world is a homogeneous play of possible phenomena, which therefore work together in the manifestation of a specific being; and behind all these masks and coincidences there stands the divine Self.

Having spoken of physical and psychic types, we are all the more obliged to take account of what we may term "eschatological types", whose order—like that of the castes—is vertical and hierarchical, not horizontal and neutral. Gnosticism—which despite its errors contains many a truth—distinguishes three fundamental types: the pneumatic, whose nature is ascending; the hylic or somatic, whose nature is descending; and the psychic, whose nature is ambiguous. Clearly, this hierarchy is independent of ordinary hierarchies, and consequently it gives rise to cases which at first glance are paradoxical; as a matter of fact, we may meet with quasi-angelic individuals among the least endowed as well as among the most gifted of men, and others who personify the opposite. This brings us back to the problem of predestination, which is intimately linked to that of initial possibilities and individual substances; of course, the divine foresight also applies to the psychic types, whose case seems to be uncertain, but who in reality "veil" their substance—and consequently their destiny—by a complex and moving fabric of contradictory and more or less superficial possibilities.

[7] All the same, if man is not responsible for his form at birth, he is to a certain degree responsible for it once he reaches his maturity, to the extent, precisely, that character can influence physical form.

Man, like the Universe, is a fabric of determination and indetermination; the latter stemming from the Infinite, and the former from the Absolute.

It may be objected that our preceding considerations on the human phenomenon are not an exposition of anthropology properly so called, since we offer no information on the "natural history" of man nor *a fortiori* on his biological origin, and so on. Now such is not our intention; we do not wish to deal with factors that escape our experience, and we are very far from accepting the "stop-gap" theory of transformist evolutionism. Original man was not a simian creature barely capable of speaking and of standing upright; he was a quasi-immaterial being enclosed in an aura still celestial, but deposited on earth; an aura similar to the "chariot of fire" of Elijah or the "cloud" that enveloped Christ during his ascension. That is to say, our conception of the origin of mankind is based on the doctrine of the projection of the archetypes *ab intra*; thus our position is that of classical emanationism—in the Neoplatonic or gnostic sense of the term—which avoids the pitfall of anthropomorphism while agreeing with the theological conception of *creatio ex nihilo*. Evolutionism for its part is the very negation of the archetypes and consequently of the divine Intellect; it is therefore the negation of an entire dimension of the real, namely that of form, of the static, of the immutable; concretely speaking, it is as if one wished to make a fabric of the wefts only, omitting the warps.

Quite obviously, an anthropology is not integral if it does not take into account the spiritual dimension of man, therefore factors such as the eschatological hierarchy of which we have just spoken, or of the analogous social functions. One cannot have *homo sapiens* without *homo religiosus*; there is no man without God.

We have stated above that man's prerogative is the capacity for objectivity, and that this is the fundamental criterion of human worth. Strictly speaking, a man is he who "knows how to think"; whoever does not know how to think, whatever his gifts may be, is not authentically a man; that is, he is not a man in the ideal sense of the term. Too many men display intelligence as long as their thought runs in the grooves of their desires, interests, and prejudices; but the moment the truth is contrary to what pleases them, their faculty of thought becomes blurred or vanishes; which is at once inhuman and "all too human". We have written in one of our books that to be objective is to die a little, unless one is a pneumatic, in which case one is dead by nature, and in that extinction finds one's life.

Thus it is important to understand that the natural virtues have an effective value only on condition of being integrated into the supernatural virtues, those precisely which presuppose a kind of death. Indeed, natural virtue does not exclude pride, that worst of logical inconsistencies, and that foremost of vices; supernatural virtue alone—rooted in God—excludes this vice which, in the eyes of Heaven, cancels all the virtues. Supernatural virtue—which alone is fully human—coincides therefore with humility; not necessarily with sentimental and individualistic humilitarianism, but with the sincere and fully justified awareness of our nothingness before God and of our relativity in relation to others. To be concrete, we shall say that a humble person is ready to accept even a partially unjust criticism if it comprises a grain of truth, and if it comes from a person who is, if not perfect, at least worthy of respect; a humble person is not interested in having his virtue recognized, he is interested in surpassing himself; hence in pleasing God more than men.

Given that our definition of *homo sapiens* is a being endowed with deiformity—which makes of him a total being, hence a theophany—then it is only logical and legitimate that, for us, the final word on anthropology is conformity to celestial norms and motion towards God; or, in other words, that the final word on anthropology be our perfection in the likeness of concentric circles and centripetal radii, both of which are set in view of the divine Center.

3. Intelligence and Character

In spirituality more than in any other domain, it is important to understand that a person's character is part of his intelligence: without a good character—a normal and therefore noble character—even a metaphysical intelligence is partially inoperative, for the simple reason that full knowledge of what lies outside us requires a full knowledge of ourselves. A person's character is, on the one hand, what he wills, and on the other hand, what he loves; will and sentiment prolong intelligence; like the intelligence—which obviously penetrates them—they are faculties of adequation. To know the Sovereign Good really is, *ipso facto*, on the one hand to will what brings us closer to it and on the other hand to love what bears witness to it; every virtue in the final analysis derives from this will and this love. Intelligence that is not accompanied by virtues gives rise to an as it were planimetric knowledge: it is as if one were to grasp but the circle or the square, and not the sphere or the cube.

—— ⁘ ——

To grasp the sphere or the cube—symbolically speaking—is to have the sense of immanence, and not merely of transcendence; and the condition of this plenitude is to know oneself, that is, to apply discernment to one's own ego, concretely and operatively since knowledge engages both will and sentiment. Sentiment in itself is not sentimentalism; it is not an abuse unless it falsifies a truth; in itself, it is the faculty of loving what is objectively lovable: the true, the holy, the beautiful, the noble; "beauty is the splendor of the true". Plenary knowledge, as we have said, requires self-knowledge: it is to discern the ambiguity, pettiness, and fragility of the ego. And it is also, and essentially, to "love one's neighbor as oneself"; that is, to see in the "other" a "myself" and in the "myself" an "other".

To have the sense of immanence—parallel to the discernment between the Real and the unreal, or between Reality that is absolute and that which is relative or contingent, or consequently between the essential and the secondary, and so on—is to have the intuition of essences, of archetypes, or let us say: of the metaphysical transparency of phenomena; and this intuition is the foundation for nobleness of soul. The noble man respects, admires, and loves owing to an essence that he perceives, whereas the vile man underestimates or scorns owing to an accident; the sense of the sacred is opposed to the instinct to disparage; the Bible speaks of "mockers". The sense of the sacred is the essence of all legitimate respect; we insist on legitimacy, for it is a question of respecting, not just anything, but what is worthy of respect; "there is no right superior to that of the truth".

To be intelligent, as everyone knows, is first of all to be able to distinguish between the essential and the secondary, to grasp the relationship between cause and effect, to adapt to either permanent or changing conditions[1] but, let us repeat—and this is far from being commonly acknowledged—that it is also to have the presentiment of the essences within things, or to glimpse the archetypes in phenomena. Intelligence may be either discriminative or contemplative, unless they are both in balance.

To have the presentiment of the essences in things: this is the basis of the Hindu *darshan*, of the visual assimilation of celestial qualities; the ideal being the coincidence between an object that manifests beauty or spirituality and a subject gifted with nobleness and depth, hence gratitude. And this is also the quasi-alchemical meaning of sacred art in all its forms.

Discernment, by its adamantine rigor, refers as it were to the mystery of the Absolute; in an analogous manner, contemplation, by its aspect of musical gentleness, pertains to the mystery of the Infinite. In the human microcosm, the volitive faculty stems as it were from the absoluteness of the Sovereign Good, whereas the affective faculty testifies to its infinitude.

—— ·:· ——

[1] Let us specify that stupidity often manifests itself through confusion between a material cause and a moral cause, or between a phenomenon due to circumstances and another resulting from a fundamental quality, in short, between an "accident" and a "substance"; for example, a government is taken for a people, or a collective psychosis for an ethnic character.

It would be easy to object that there are men who are intelligent while being bad, and that there are men who are good without being intelligent; now we do not contest that a morally imperfect man can be intelligent, we merely contest that his intelligence can be complete and thus enjoy a multidimensional infallibility. As for men who are morally sound but intellectually ungifted, they are never stupid, for virtue excludes stupidity pure and simple; no doubt their intelligence is more contemplative than discriminative, but it is real, virtue being precisely a mode of spiritual adequation, hence of intelligence in the essential sense of the term; and naivety is not stupidity.

What is in any case striking in virtuous people, even in those who are but modestly gifted, is that they always have good sense; in this they can be distinctly superior to certain philosophers who, while being clever and ingenious, yet are strangely lacking in the sense of the real. Many proverbs testify to a popular wisdom that doubtless has nothing Aristotelian about it, but which by way of compensation comes close to the angelically simple and concrete language of the Bible.

—— ·⁝· ——

The ideal for *homo sapiens* is the combination of a perfect intelligence with a perfect character, and this is the proper meaning of the word "wisdom"; it is the ideal represented by gnosis, which *a priori* is concerned with the restoration of man's primordial perfection. Esoterism is so to speak the "religion of intelligence": this means that it operates with the intellect—and not with sentiment and will only—and that as a result its content is all that intelligence can attain, and that it alone can attain.[2] The "subject" of esoterism is the Intellect and its "object" is *ipso facto* total Truth, namely—expressed in Vedantic terms—the

[2] Not all historical esoterism is esoterism pure and simple, far from it; an exegesis colored by confessional bias, or overly involved in mystical subjectivism is hardly true gnosis. On the other hand, it is far from being the case that all that one fits into the category of esoterism pertains to it: too often it happens that in dealing with this subject authors make no distinction between what is genuine and what is counterfeit, thus between truth and error; this is in keeping with the two sins of our time which are the replacement of intelligence by psychology and the confusion between the psychic and the spiritual.

doctrine of *Ātmā* and *Māyā*; and to speak of *Ātmā* and *Māyā* is thereby to speak of *Jnāna*, direct knowledge, intellectual intuition.

To say that man is made of intelligence, will, and sentiment, means that he is made for the Truth, the Way, and Virtue. In other words, intelligence is made for comprehension of the True; will, for concentration on the Sovereign Good; and sentiment, for conformity to the True and the Good. Instead of "sentiment", we could also say "soul" or "faculty of loving", for this is a fundamental dimension of man; not a weakness as it is all too often thought, but a participation in the divine nature, in conformity with the mystery that "God is Love".

All things considered, only the *sophia perennis* can be considered a total good without reservations; exoterism, with its obvious limitations, always comprises an aspect of "lesser evil" owing to its inevitable concessions to collective human nature, hence to the intellectual, moral, and spiritual possibilities of a human average that by definition is "fallen"; "God alone is good", Christ said. From the operative even more than from the speculative point of view, exoterism places pure intelligence between brackets, as it were: it replaces it with belief and the reasonings linked to belief, which means that it puts emphasis on will and sentiment. It must do so, given its mission and its reason for being; but this limitation is nonetheless a double-edged sword whose consequences are not as purely positive as religious prejudice would have it. It is true that the ambiguity of exoterism is not unrelated to the designs of Providence.

Impious intelligence is incomparably worse than pious stupidity; *corruptio optimi pessima*. In itself, intelligence is "pious" because its very substance is pure discernment, and pure contemplation, of the Sovereign Good; a true intelligence is inconceivable outside that already celestial quality which is the sense of the sacred; the love of God being the very essence of virtue. In a word, intelligence, to the very extent that it is faithful to its nature and its vocation, produces or favors the moral qualities; conversely, virtue, under the same conditions, necessarily opens onto wholeness of mind, hence onto knowledge of the Real.

4. The Primacy of Intellection

It has been said that the proof of an affirmation is incumbent on him who enunciates the thesis, not upon him who rejects it; but this is a perfectly arbitrary opinion, for if we are owed a proof for a positive affirmation, we are equally owed one for a negative affirmation; it is not the positive character of the affirmation, it is the absoluteness of its character that obliges us to prove it, whether its content is positive or negative. There is no need to prove an inexistence that one supposes, but one is obliged to prove an inexistence that one affirms. It is true that those who deny the supernatural do not lack arguments which in their eyes are proofs of their opinion, but nonetheless they imagine that their opinion is a natural axiom that requires no demonstration; this is rationalist legalism, not pure logic. Theists, on the contrary, feel that it is normal to support by proofs the reality of the Invisible, except when they speak *pro domo*, basing themselves upon the evidence of faith or gnosis.

The ontological proof of God—expressed by Saint Augustine and developed by Saint Anselm—has often been misinterpreted, starting already in the Middle Ages. The fact is that it does not signify that God is real because He can be conceived, but on the contrary that He can be conceived because He is real: in other words, the reality of God entails, for our intellective faculty, certitude concerning that reality, and this certitude in its turn entails, for our rational faculty, the possibility to conceive of the Absolute. And it is precisely this possibility of reason—and *a fortiori* the pre-rational intuition of the intellect—which constitutes the prerogative that characterizes man.

The error, in the critique of the ontological proof of God, consists in not seeing that to imagine some object or other is in no wise the same as to conceive of the absolute, or the Absolute as such; for what matters here is not the subjective play of our mind, but essentially the absolute Object which determines it and which, in the final analysis, even constitutes the very reason for the existence of human intelligence. Without a real God, man is not possible.

In speaking of the ontological argument, we have in mind the essential thesis and not the partly problematical reasonings which are supposed to uphold it. Fundamentally, the basis of the argument is the analogy between the macrocosm-metacosm and the microcosm, or between God and the soul: in a certain respect, we are That which is, and consequently we can know all that is, and thus Being as such; for if in one respect there is the relationship of incommensurability, there is also the relationship of analogy and even of identity, otherwise we would be nothingness pure and simple. The principle of knowledge does not of itself imply any limitation; to know is to know all that is knowable, and the knowable coincides with the real, given that *a priori* and in the Absolute the subject and the object are indistinguishable: to know is to be, and conversely. This brings us to the Arabic saying: "He who knoweth his soul, knoweth his Lord"; without forgetting the injunction of the oracle at Delphi: "Know thyself". If we are told that the Absolute is unknowable, this applies, not to our intellective faculty as such, but to a particular *de facto* modality of this faculty; to a particular husk, not to the substance.

In the domain of human thought there are few things more pathetic than the need to "prove" *Ātmā* or *Māyā*; for to say that these two things—"if they exist"—are absolutely remote is to say implicitly that they are absolutely near; too near, in a certain sense, to be provable. The following is a fallacious argument: since everything that is not the Absolute—"supposing that it exists"—is enclosed in *Māyā*, how can we know the Absolute, and consequently the Relative as such, given that our knowledge quite obviously is confined within *Māyā*? Our reply—and it follows from our preceding considerations—is that neither of these two notions pertains absolutely to *Māyā*: the first because its very content situates it outside Illusion, even though the notion *qua* notion obviously pertains to the illusory order; and the same holds true for the second notion, that of *Māyā*, precisely: if it pertains necessarily to Illusion as an intellectual or mental phenomenon, it is nonetheless linked to *Ātmā* since it exists only with respect to it; without *Ātmā*, no *Māyā* is possible. This amounts to saying that the notion of Illusion is a ray of *Ātmā* entering into *Māyā*, in a less direct fashion no doubt than is the case for the notion of *Ātmā*, but nonetheless in a real, or relatively real, manner. We could also say that the notion of the Real is real, or that the notion of the Absolute is absolute, in the same way that it has been said that "the doctrine of Unity is unique". The idea of the illusory, of the relative or the contingent, is linked to that of the Real and benefits from the same logical and ontological rule.

All in all, the proof of the pure logician is based on a starting point that is "contrary to nature"—if man is viewed in his primordial and normative integrity—that is to say, it is based on an ignorance and a doubt which, precisely, are not normal to man as such; the argumentation of the pure metaphysician on the contrary—even if he happens to employ the language of the logician as a dialectical stratagem—is founded, not upon doubt, but upon analogy and, more profoundly, upon identity both intellectual and existential. If, analogically speaking, Reality is the geometric point, the knowledge that we have of it corresponds either to the concentric circles or to the radii which are both centrifugal and centripetal, for on the one hand Truth emanates from the Real, and on the other hand Knowledge extends to the Real. The point, the circle, the radius, and also the spiral: these are the graphic symbols of Knowledge, whatever the symbol—or relation—that predominates according to the aspect considered.

Ramanuja and others have maintained that the Shankarian doctrine of the two "hypostases" of the divine Self—*Brahma* as such and *Brahma* as *Māyā*—is false because it introduces, it would seem, an unintelligible and irreducible duality into the Absolute; but this is an artificial argument, because it considers only one aspect of the problem, while deliberately neglecting another which is the key. The absolute Self is pure Subject; now contingent subjects too are nothing if not subjectivity or consciousness, and it is in this respect, and not with respect to contingency—or projection and reverberation—that *Brahma* or *Ātmā* is one and indivisible. As for *Māyā*, it proceeds necessarily from the very nature of *Ātmā*—on pain of being a pure impossibility—and it proves the Infinitude, All-Possibility, and Radiation of *Ātmā*; *Māyā* exteriorizes and unfolds the innumerable potentialities of *Ātmā*. *Māyā* cannot not be, and to deny it is not to know the nature of the supreme Self.

—— ·:· ——

To ask for the proof of intellection—hence of a direct, adequate, and infallible knowledge of the supernatural—is to prove that one does not have access to it, and it is, analogically speaking, to ask for the proof of the adequacy of our elementary sensations, which no one doubts, on pain of not being able to live. But the absence of metaphysical intellection in most men of the "iron age" does not for all that close the door to the salvific supernatural, as is shown by the phenomenon of revelation, and the subsequent phenomenon of faith, both of which presuppose a kind of elementary—but in no way insufficient—intuition, which we could term "moral" and sometimes even "aesthetic"; for in fact, the reality of God penetrates all our being. To doubt this is to make of oneself "a house divided against itself".

In fact, when God is removed from the universe, it becomes a desert of rock-strewn debris or of ice; it is deprived of life and warmth, and any man who still has a sense of the integrally real refuses to admit that this should be reality; for if reality were made of rocks, there would be no place in the universe for flowers, or any beauty or sweetness whatsoever. Similarly for the soul: remove faith—including that element of faith that forms part of gnosis—and the soul becomes impoverished, chilled, rigid, and embittered; or it falls into a hedonism unworthy of the human state; moreover, the one does not preclude the other, for blind passions always cover a heart of ice, a heart that is "dead" in fact. Thus, there is an ostentatious and "humanitarian" charity which, at bottom, is no more than the psychological compensation for spiritual bitterness or hatred of God.

Be that as it may, pure rationalism[1] wants to pass itself off as being the quintessence of "exact thought", or for the only thought that can be exact, for exactitude as such; however, it must not be forgotten that rationalism, or the "criticism" which systematizes it, comprises arbitrary and practically pseudo-mystical arguments, such as the Kantian barb aimed at the intuitive certitudes of the believer: to have recourse to this certitude is, it would appear, "to make quite abusively an objective reality out of a subjective ideality"; now whence does this philosopher know that this "ideality" is not a reality? He speaks of the "rapturous illusion" (*schwärmerischer Wahn*) which would consist in knowing supernatural entities via our sentiment; by what right does he speak thus, since he has never experienced said sentiment? This brings

[1] This epithet is not a tautology, since Aristotle and even Plato are readily numbered among the rationalists, when in fact they never claimed to draw everything from reason alone.

us back to the opinion according to which he who denies an affirmation does not have to prove his negation, given—it would appear—that only he who affirms something is required to provide a proof for his affirmation; as if the peremptory negation of something which one does not know were not an affirmation in its turn! Moreover, how can one not see from the outset the initial contradiction of criticism, namely the illusion of being able to define the limitations—clearly conjectural—of reason starting from reason itself. It is to wish to enunciate rules—analogically speaking—about the possible limitations of the optic nerve with the help of the visual faculty; or it is to wish to hear hearing, or to grasp with the hand the capacity of grasping.[2]

Nevertheless, the possibility of determining the limits of reason does exist; but it exists only starting from—and by means of—the pure intellect, hence precisely from what Kantian criticism, without the shadow of a proof, flatly denies. We will perhaps be told—although this would mean sidestepping the issue—that criticism has long been obsolete, and that it is not worth fighting the dead; no doubt it has been obsolete philosophically and in a literary sense, but not practically, for it survives by its fruits, or by its fruit, namely the quasi-official abolition of speculative intelligence, which in the final analysis means: the abolition of specifically human intelligence, or of intelligence pure and simple.

Pascal's wager is not, after all, to be disdained; what gives it all its force are not merely the arguments in favor of God and our immortality, but also the importance—quantitative as well as qualitative—of the voices in favor of these two capital notions, that of God and that of our soul; we have in mind here the power and majesty of the sacred Scriptures and the host of innumerable sages and saints. If these great men are not qualified to speak in the name of man, then there is no such thing as man.

[2] In order to discredit faith and seduce believers, Kant does not hesitate to appeal to pride or vanity: whoever does not rely on reason alone is a "minor" who refuses to "grow up"; if men allow themselves to be led by "authorities" instead of "thinking for themselves", it is solely due to laziness and cowardice, no more no less. A thinker who needs to make use of such means—which finally are "demagogic"—must truly be short of serious arguments.

5. Gnosis Is Not Just Anything

It is a fact that too many authors—we would almost say: general opinion—attribute to gnosis what is proper to Gnosticism and to other counterfeits of the *sophia perennis*, and moreover make no distinction between the latter and the most fanciful movements, such as spiritualism, theosophism, and the pseudo-esoterisms that saw the light of day in the twentieth century. It is particularly regrettable that these confusions are taken seriously by most theologians, who obviously have an interest in entertaining the worst opinion possible concerning gnosis; now the fact that an imposture necessarily imitates a good, since otherwise it could not even exist, does not authorize us to accuse the good with all the sins of the imitation.

In reality, gnosis is essentially the path of the intellect and thus of intellection; the motive force of this path is above all intelligence, not will and sentiment as is the case in the Semitic monotheistic mysticisms—including average Sufism. Gnosis is characterized by its recourse to pure metaphysics: the distinction between *Ātmā* and *Māyā* and the consciousness of the potential identity between the human subject, *jīvātmā*, and the Divine Subject, *Paramātmā*. The path comprises on the one hand "understanding", and on the other "concentration"; hence doctrine and method. The modalities of the method are quite diverse: in particular, there is on the one hand the *mantra*, which is the evocative and transforming formula, and on the other hand, the *yantra*, the visual symbol. The path is the passage from potentiality to virtuality, and from virtuality to actuality, its summit being the state of the one "delivered in this life", the *jīvan-mukta*.

As for Gnosticism, whether it arises in a Christian, Muslim, or other climate, it is a fabric of more or less delirious speculations, often of Manichean origin; and it is a mythomania characterized by a dangerous mixture of exoteric and esoteric concepts. Doubtless it contains symbolisms that are not without interest—the contrary would be astonishing—but it is said that "the road to hell is paved with good intentions"; it could just as well be said that it is paved with symbolisms.

It may be remarked, perhaps, that in gnosis as well as in Gnosticism, "enlightenment" plays a preponderant role; but this is to confuse "enlightenment" with intellection, or the latter with the former; whereas in reality intellection is active, and enlightenment, passive, whatever the level of the experiences involved may be. This is not to say that the phenomenon of enlightenment does not arise in the climate of gnosis; it does so necessarily, but not by way of method or as a point of reference. An analogous remark could be made regarding hermeneutics, that is, the interpretation of sacred Scriptures; no doubt commentary on the Scriptures is practiced in the climate of gnosis—for example, it goes without saying that the *Upanishads* have been commented upon—but this is quite different from the far-removed and unverifiable interpretation of scriptural formulas whose literal meanings do not at all indicate what the mystical exegetes try to draw from them—with the aid of "enlightenment", precisely.[1]

It is true that the word "enlightenment" can have a higher meaning, in which case it no longer designates a passive phenomenon; unitive and liberating enlightenment is beyond the distinction between passivity and activity. Or more exactly, enlightenment is the divine Activity in us, but for that very reason it also possesses an aspect of supreme Passivity in the sense that it coincides with the "extinction" of the passional and dark elements separating man from his immanent divine Essence; this extinction constituting receptivity to the Influx of Heaven—without losing sight of the fact that the divine Order comprises a "Passive Perfection" as well as an "Active Perfection", and that the human spirit must in the final analysis participate in both mysteries.

In gnosis, there is first of all the intellective knowledge of the Absolute—not merely of the "personal God"—and then self-knowledge; for one cannot know the divine Order without knowing oneself. "Know thyself", says the inscription over the portal of the initiatic temple at Delphi; and "the Kingdom of God is within you".

Just as the ether is present in each of the sensible elements, such as fire and water, and just as intelligence is present in each of the mental faculties, such as imagination and memory, so too gnosis is necessarily present in each of the great religions, whether we grasp its traces or not.

[1] We do not contest that a word or an image in a sacred text may have a meaning that cannot be divined at a first reading; but in such cases this meaning cannot be contrary to the literal meaning or incompatible with the context.

We have said that the motive force of the path of gnosis is intelligence; now this principle is very far from being applicable to a spiritual society—unless it is not very numerous—for in general, intelligence is largely inoperative once it is called upon to hold a collectivity in balance; in all justice, one cannot deny that sentimental and humilitarian moralism has a certain realism and hence a corresponding efficacy. It follows from all this, not that gnosis has to repudiate socially its principle of the primacy of intelligence, but that it must put each thing in its place and take men as they are; that is precisely why the perspective of gnosis will be the first to insist, not upon a simplifying moralism, but upon intrinsic virtue, which—like beauty—is "the splendor of the true". Intelligence must be not only objective and conceptual, but also subjective and existential; the oneness of the object demands the totality of the subject.

When one has experienced the pious sophistries typical of voluntaristic and moralistic doctrines, it becomes quite clear that gnosis is not a luxury, and that it alone can extricate us from the impasses of the "alternativism" that is part and parcel of the confessional spirit. There is, for instance, the stupefying thesis of the Asharites, according to which there are no natural causes: fire burns, not because it is in its nature to burn, but because, each time something burns, it is God who intervenes directly and who "creates" the burning.[2] Ibn Rushd pertinently objects—against Ghazzali, who made this holy absurdity his own—that "if something did not have its specific nature, it would have no name proper to it. . . . Intelligence is nothing else than the perception of causes . . . and whoever denies causes must also deny the intellect".

What the Asharites have not understood—and this is characteristic of the "alternativism" of exoteric thought—is that natural causes, such as the function of fire to burn, in no way exclude immanent

[2] Equally anti-metaphysical is the Christian opinion that the hypostases are neither substances nor modes, that they are merely "relations" and yet that they are persons. It is appropriate to distinguish between the Trinity and trinitarian theology, and no less so between Unity and unitarian theology.

supernatural causality,[3] any more than the limited subjectivity of the creature excludes the immanence of the absolute Subject. Immanent divine causality is "vertical" and supernatural, whereas cosmic causality is "horizontal" and natural, or in other words: the first is comparable to centrifugal radii, and the second to concentric circles. It is this combination of two relationships or of two perspectives that characterizes integrally metaphysical thought, hence gnosis.[4]

There is intelligence and intelligence, knowledge and knowledge; there is on the one hand a fallible mind that registers and elaborates, and on the other hand a heart-intellect that perceives and projects its infallible vision onto thought. Here lies the entire difference between a logical certitude that can replace another logical certitude, and a quasi-ontological certitude that nothing can replace because it is what we are, or because we are what it is.

[3] According to the Koran, God ordered the fire that was to burn Abraham: "Be coolness. . . !" which would be meaningless if the nature of fire were not to burn, and which therefore refutes *a priori* and divinely the Asharite opinion.

[4] It should be noted that, just as there is a "relatively absolute"—the logical absurdity of this formulation does not preclude its ontologically plausible meaning—so too is there a "naturally supernatural", and this is precisely the permanent divine intervention, by virtue of immanence, in cosmic causality.

II.

ONTOLOGY AND COSMOLOGY

1. Universal Categories

Aristotle, in erecting his table of categories—substance, quantity, quality, relation, activity, passivity, place, moment, position, condition—seems to have been more concerned about the rational classification of things than about their concrete nature.[1] However, since our own standpoint is closer to cosmology than to Peripatetic logic—although the boundaries fluctuate—we shall give preference to the following enumeration: object and subject, space and time (which are container-categories); matter and energy, form and number (which are content-categories); quality and quantity, simplicity and complexity (which are attribute-categories); the first term of each couple is static, and the second, dynamic, approximately and symbolically speaking. This being granted, we cannot exclude other possible angles of vision, whether they are more analytic, or on the contrary more synthetic—but always prefigured by some symbolism of nature.[2]

This is not to say that all of the categories are equal: thus, space is related rather to the "being" of things, and time, to their "becoming"; at the beginning of a human cycle—in the "golden age"—it is somehow space that predominates, whereas at the end of the cycle, it is time. Likewise, form prevails over number, just as quality takes precedence over quantity; and so too, matter takes precedence over energy, just as "existing" takes precedence over "doing", but one could no doubt also say the reverse, by opposing the "subtle" to the "gross". As for the categories subject and object, they are ontologically, and therefore qualitatively, interchangeable: the whole question is to know on which of the poles the emphasis is placed, that is to say, on which side God or His reflection is situated.[3]

[1] The Greek word *kategoria*, "argument", means in the last analysis: an ultimate form of thought, that is to say a key-notion capable of classifying other notions, or even all the notions having a bearing on existence.

[2] Mention should be made of this fundamental enumeration: space, time, form, number, matter—fundamental because of its relation to the symbolism of the pentagram, the human body, the hand, the five elements. There are some who put "life" in place of matter, thinking no doubt of energy, which penetrates everything.

[3] The *Vedānta* puts the whole emphasis on the absolute "Self", whereas the religions envisage above all the "God-Object", that is to say the "absolutely other".

It is not possible to give one simple and definitive answer to the question of knowing how many existential categories there are.[4] The lines of demarcation in this matter are both precise and vague: on the one hand, the number of categories chosen in terms of any particular definition is precise, but the defining perspectives are diverse; on the other hand, and outside such perspectives or systems, the number of categories is unlimited, as is that of phenomena. Color for example is a category which embraces all possible colors; but any particular color is a new category and it encompasses all of its own shades, but not those of other colors; which amounts to saying that everything involving modalities—or insofar as it involves them—may be considered as being a category. In this way the Aristotelian category of "relation" is the denominator of an indefinite series of other conceivable categories, such as cause and effect, reality and possibility,[5] potentiality and actuality, necessity and liberty, activity and passivity, container and content, excess and privation; the latter *distinguo* being moreover the point of departure of Peripatetic ethics, which consists in choosing the golden mean.

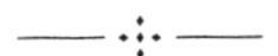

The Greeks, and after them Saint Augustine, taught that it is in the nature of the Good (*Agathon*) to impart itself; that is what explains the presence, at every level of the Universe, of an existential system composed of containers, contents, and modalities, *ad majorem Dei gloriam.*

The notion of the Good which we have just mentioned allows us to come back once again—for we have already discussed this elsewhere—to the crucial problem of evil. The distant and indirect cause of what we rightly call evil—namely privation of the good—is the mystery of All-Possibility; that is to say, being infinite, All-Possibility necessarily encompasses the possibility of its own negation, thus the

[4] Aristotle indicates ten, but elsewhere only mentions three: substance, quality, relationship.

[5] There is no reason for objecting here that the possible is also real in its own order, because it goes without saying that from the standpoint of the distinction in question, "real" is a synonym of "effective" or "effectuated".

"possibility of the impossible" or the "being of nothingness". This paradoxical possibility, this "possibility of the absurd"—since it exists and since nothing can exist outside of the Good, which coincides with Being—has of necessity a positive function, which is to manifest the Good—or all good things—by means of contrast; it does so both in "time" or succession as well as in "space" or coexistence. In "space", evil opposes the good and thereby heightens the latter's luster or brings out its nature *a contrario*; in "time", the cessation of evil manifests the victory of the good, in accordance with the principle that *vincit omnia Veritas*; the two modes demonstrate the "unreality" of evil and at the same time its illusory character. In other words: since the function of evil is the contrasting manifestation of the good and also of the latter's final victory, we shall say that evil by its very nature is condemned to its own negation; representing either the "spatial" or "temporal" absence of the good, evil thus returns to this absence, which is privation of being and hence nothingness. If one were to object that the good is likewise perishable, we would answer that it returns to its celestial or divine prototype, solely within which it is wholly "itself"; what is perishable in the good is not the good in itself, it is this or that covering which limits it. As we have said more than once—and this brings us back to the root of the question—evil is a necessary consequence of remoteness from the divine Sun, the "overflowing" source of the cosmogonic trajectory;[6] the mystery of mysteries being All-Possibility as such.

A remark is necessary here: one might object that evil likewise, by its very nature, tends to impart itself; that is true, but it has this tendency precisely because it is opposed to the radiation of the good and thus cannot help imitating the latter in some fashion. For evil is by definition both opposition and imitation: within the framework of opposition it is ontologically forced to imitate; "the more they blaspheme the more they praise God", said Meister Eckhart. Evil, insofar as it exists, partakes in the good represented by existence.

[6] Evil—the "serpent" of Paradise—rose out of nothingness as soon as the interior world of the primordial androgyne became exteriorized; now this cosmogonic moment coincides with the creation of Eve, and thus with the scission of the still immaterial androgyne who was the "first Adam". The materialization, or Fall, came after the exteriorization and under the influence of the serpent; individualism—an elementary mode of "luciferianism"—caused the imprisonment in matter, with all the subsequent calamities, but also with the appropriate graces.

Good and evil are not, strictly speaking, existential categories in the way the object, the subject, space, and time are; for the good is the very being of things—manifested by the categories precisely—which means that the things are finally "modes of the good"; whereas evil indicates paradoxically the absence of this being, while annexing certain things or certain characteristics at the level accessible to it and owing to predispositions allowing it to do so. But despite this reservation, one may consider good and evil as existential categories for the following reasons: the good includes on the one hand all that manifests the qualities of the divine Principle, and on the other hand all things inasmuch as they manifest this same Principle by their existence, and also inasmuch as they fulfill a necessary ontological function. Evil for its part includes all that manifests a privation from the standpoint of the qualities or from that of Being itself; it is harmful in various ways, even were this harmfulness to be neutralized and compensated, in given cases, by positive factors. That is to say that there are things which are bad or harmful in principle but not in fact, just as there are others which are good and benefic in the same way;[7] all of which contributes to the unfolding of the cosmic play with its innumerable combinations.

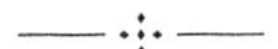

Regarding the categories "subject" and "object", we shall begin by taking note of the fact that the object is reality in itself, or reality envisaged in connection with its perceptibility, whereas the subject is consciousness in itself, or consciousness envisaged in relation to its faculty of perception. Now in both cases there is a relationship of reciprocity and a relationship of divergence. With respect to the first relationship, we would say that the world, insofar as it is a perception, is part of the subject, which perceives it; conversely the ego, insofar as it is something which the subject perceives—namely as something outside itself—is part of the object; in the second case, that of divergence, we oppose the "in itself", which is evidently objective, to pure consciousness "withdrawn into itself"; in the last analysis this brings

[7] Because there is, for example, the physical ugliness of a good man, and the physical beauty of a bad man.

us back to transcendence and to immanence, which meet in Unity and in the Indivisible.

On the plane of intellectual, or even of simply rational, knowledge, the complementarity "object-subject" is the parallelism between being and thought, the thing and the notion, the formal situation and the notional adequation; this is what constitutes the foundation of Aristotelian logic—or simply of logic as such—the key to which is the syllogism. Let us remark on this occasion that modern men, when they speak of "object" and "subject", tend to think that the former is unknowable and that the latter is incapable of exact knowledge; in other words, they like to evoke the specters of the "thing in itself" (*das Ding an sich*) and the supposed inadequacy of cognition. In reality, knowledge of the contingent and the relative is necessarily contingent and relative; not in the sense that it would not be adequate—because adequation is the very reason for being of knowledge—but in the sense that we can only perceive one aspect of the object at a time, and this depends on our standpoint, that of the subject, precisely. Only knowledge of the Absolute is absolute, and it is so because, in gnosis, the Absolute knows itself in the depths of the human subject; this is the whole mystery of divine immanence in the microcosm.

What we have just said evidently implies that there is not only the physical object—sensorial or psychic—there is also the meta-physical Object which confers on the world, and thus on what the world contains, all of its reality and all of its meaning. If the object is "the other", the first "Other" is the transcendent Principle, and that is how the notion of the objective embraces, on the one hand, all that is and, on the other hand, the only One that is. And likewise, *mutatis mutandis*, for the notion of the subjective: if on the one hand the subject is the ego both psychic and sensorial, on the other hand it is the Intellect and the immanent Logos, which is the pure Knower and whose consciousness extends in principle from the human ego to the Divine Self.

The relatively "other" and the relatively "oneself" obviously constitute a complementary opposition; whereas the "absolutely Other" and the "absolutely Oneself" coincide. Here one could object that there is also the confrontation between the "relatively oneself", namely the ego, and the "absolutely Other", namely God; but in point of fact the God with whom we can be the interlocutor is not the "absolutely Other", or is so only in a "relatively absolute" sense. And if we are able to conceive of the pure Absolute, that is because our Intellect, which is "uncreated and uncreatable", penetrates "to the very depths of God"; once again, the Transcendent and the Immanent are One and the same. Liberating Knowledge consists in grasping the implication of the nature of things, because it is in the nature of things that we should understand what these entail.

All this amounts to saying that the cosmic object—the world—is as if suspended between two complementary dimensions, transcendence and immanence: on the one hand, God is the "Other" who is infinitely "above" the world, and on the other hand, the world is His manifestation in which He is present; this implies, on the one hand, that without this immanence the world would be reduced to nothing, and, on the other hand, that the world—and all that it contains—is necessarily symbolical. In a certain sense, nothing resembles God, but in another sense, everything resembles Him, at least with respect to positive manifestation, not negative manifestation. Likewise, the human subject—the ego—is as though suspended between "elevation" and "depth": between the divine Being which resides "in the Heavens", and the divine Self which resides "in the depths of the heart". The first is the separative perspective, that of adoration, worship, law, obedience, in short, of religion; the second is the unitive perspective, that of wisdom and union; or that of pure sanctity, which by definition is "being" and not merely "thought".

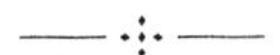

The nature of things requires an equilibrium between a theosophy which is positive and another which is negative; between a perspective—or way of approach—either cataphatic or apophatic. God knows Himself; we would even say: He "is" knowledge of Himself, and He can project this knowledge into man, without our being able to say on that account that man as such knows God. In any case, the distinction between a conceptualization that is either positive or negative—either inclusive or exclusive—can take place only on the plane of thought or expression, not on that of pure intellection, which essentially transcends the scission between subject and object.

One should not purely and simply confuse consciousness as such with the subject, and existence as such with the object; because the subject exists, and the object contains phenomena of consciousness.

Furthermore there seems to be a considerable asymmetry between existence and consciousness, because—as we have just said—the latter is included in the former, while the former—existence—is not necessarily conscious; however, existing things need a witness in order to fully exist: in a certain sense, an unconscious object is nothing without a subject perceiving it; the raw existence of the inanimate object being no more than a sort of virtuality.[8]

Space differentiates and conserves; time changes and transforms. The importance of certain symbolisms obliges us to mention here things which are only too evident at first sight, but which are in fact rarely examined in depth; namely, and first of all, that space has three objective dimensions: length, width, and height; then six subjective dimensions: above, below, right, left, before, behind. Analogously, time has four objective dimensions—the four phases of the cycle: morning, day, evening, night; or spring, summer, autumn, winter; or again, childhood, youth, maturity, old age—and two subjective dimensions: the past and the future; the present being beyond our grasp, as is the center in space. All of these elements give rise to various analogies, on the plane of the spiritual or simply moral life as well as on that of ontology or cosmology.

It should be pointed out that space and time—those which we know through experience[9]—include psychic as well as physical phenomena, but do not reach the domain of the spirit. Psychic elements can in fact fix themselves in a given place and have a given duration; this could never happen with an idea, a knowledge, a principle as such.

[8] Pascal said, in substance, that we are minute, but that we know it, whereas the universe in incommensurable, but it does not know it.

[9] Because there are others, each category being merely a manifestation—at a given cosmic level—of a universal principle. In our book *Résumé de métaphysique intégrale* (chapter on creation) we specified that "the Hindu conceptions are often more indicative than systematically consistent", having in mind the fact that space and time are presented as being integral parts of "pure" or divine *Māyā*; taken literally, this would imply that terrestrial things are situated, by virtue of their contents, in the divine Order; but, symbolically or "indicatively" speaking, this seemingly restrictive language is sufficient.

Let us mention here that instead of speaking of "space" and "time", we could also—as Aristotle does—speak of "place" and "moment", thereby emphasizing their concrete application, but to the detriment of the general notions. This can easily be seen from the following considerations: there is a relationship, on the one hand, between matter and space and, on the other, between energy and time: matter is quintessentially ether, which is identified in fact with space, while energy is conceivable—at least in act—only within time because it coincides practically with change.

Transposed into time, the point—a spatial symbol—signifies the instant; psychologically and spiritually speaking, it is concentration. The circle expresses not only spatial infinitude, but also eternity—infinitude, because it prolongs the center and evokes concentric circles repeating themselves without limit, and eternity because it has neither beginning nor end. The circle evokes the roundness of the celestial vault and that of the horizon, and it is thus an image of space; in an analogous manner, the square evokes the four phases of the annual cycle; consequently it can be an image of time. In space, quaternity signifies stability; in time, it signifies movement; in spirituality, progressive movement as well as qualitative stability are conditions *sine qua non* of realization. Thus it is that numerical and geometrical symbols have their applications not only in space, but also in time; as they have them—and even *a priori*—on the ontological, cosmological, and spiritual planes, of which the cosmic planes are only projections.

Time like space contains matter, energy, form, and number; nevertheless one may say that matter is closer to space, and energy closer to time. Space equals the ether which fills it and which is the basic matter from which the four other elements and all the substances are derived; and time equals change, and thus the energy which provokes it. To speak of "matter" is to speak of "crystallization" or "coagulation"; to speak of "energy" is to speak of "vibration".

Regarding the category "form"—considered *a priori* in its physical mode—one must distinguish first of all the forms that are two-dimensional from those that are three-dimensional, namely distinguish figures from volumes;[10] then we perceive the diversity of circular, triangular, and other forms, in short all the geometrical possibilities, irregular as well as regular; not forgetting, on an entirely different plane, the difference—irrespective of our tastes—between arbitrary and necessary forms, beautiful and ugly, as well as noble and vile, depending on whether their contents are positive or privative.

In the domain of numbers, one distinguishes first of all between even and odd numbers; the latter refer to unity and evoke the return to the principle, and the former signify projection and therefore increasing remoteness. Next, one distinguishes between whole numbers, which repeat or increase unity, and fractions, which divide it, the former referring to manifestation or effectuation, and the latter—which remain within unity—to the principle or to potentiality. Finally, another distinction is that between numbers which are simply quantitative, and those which are symbolical and qualitative, the latter—such as duality, trinity, quaternity—being equivalent to the fundamental geometric figures and the Pythagorean numbers.

And this is important: there is an analogy on the one hand between the positive or active principle and odd numbers, and on the other between the negative or passive principle and even numbers; this is the couple *Yang* and *Yin* which determines all oppositions and all complementarities—the complementarities being unitive, such as active and passive, masculine and feminine, and the oppositions being separative, such as positive and negative, good and evil. The odd numbers are centripetal, they bring things back to Unity—as stated above—and consequently represent it in the mode of plurality; whereas the even numbers are centrifugal, for they represent projection into the multiple and indefinite. But since the two principles, *Yin* as well as *Yang*, have come forth out of *Tao*—their prefiguration in *Tao* being respectively Infinitude and Absoluteness—they are bound to manifest their underlying unity on the very plane of their divergence, and that is what the *Yin-Yang* sign indicates, where the black part includes a white point, and conversely; in other words, masculinity involves an element of femininity, and femininity an element of masculinity, and each pole possesses, to varying degrees, a function

[10] Transposed to other orders, the difference between planimetric and three-dimensional geometry is equivalent to that between the abstract and the concrete, theory and practice, program and realization, truth and reality, doctrine and sanctity.

that is positive and another that is negative. In the first case—as we have remarked more than once—the masculine element refers to the Absolute, and the feminine to the Infinite; in the second case, there is in masculinity a danger of contraction and hardening, and in femininity, on the contrary, a tendency to an exteriorization that is dissolving and indefinite. Let us add finally—and this demonstrates in its own way the compensatory reciprocity just mentioned—that in geometrical symbolism, *Yang* is represented by surfaces which mark out boundaries, "enclose", and thus connect with unity; whereas *Yin* is represented by stars—of three or more branches—which project and "radiate"; all this independently of the question of odd or even numbers.[11] This whole digression on a Far-Eastern symbol is justified here by the fact that it implies a numerical dimension, or more precisely a doctrine of duality.

There is something quasi-divine about the first four numbers, and likewise about the first four forms, because they are incomparable, on the one hand among themselves and on the other in relation to all the other numbers and all the other forms. The point, the line, the triangle, the square are fundamentally differentiated as if each one constituted a separate species, whereas the subsequent forms, starting with the pentagon, all seem to belong to one and the same species; moreover their series rapidly ends in the circle,[12] since one cannot imagine a regular polygon having a hundred or a thousand angles: already the dodecagon gives the impression of being "out of breath". There is thus something quasi-absolute in the first four forms as in the first four numbers; they are symbols which are properly speaking hypostatic, whereas the number five, together with the pentagon or the pentagram—or the

[11] In an analogous but less direct manner, the Swastika expresses in a "star" form and in centrifugal mode what the *Yin-Yang* and its derivatives represent in a "surface" form and in centripetal mode. This question has been examined in one of the treatises on symbolist archeology of the German Emperor Wilhelm II (*Die chinesische Monade*); in the same pamphlet, the author remarks that "this dualism (*Yin* and *Yang*) is fundamentally distinct from that of the Persians as it was taught by Zoroaster and later by Manicheism, because for the latter the combat between the two principles is supposed to end in the victory of light, whereas in China *Yin* and *Yang* . . . represent a harmonious and balanced relationship".

[12] In fact, the circle symbolizes totality, just as the point symbolizes unity or unicity; all the other geometrical figures or numerical values are situated between these two poles.

five-branched star—seems to inaugurate the world, the creation, the cosmos, while referring necessarily to prototypes *in divinis*. In other words, it is the first four numbers and the first four forms which have so to speak the privilege of being able to "define" or "describe" pure Being; and this is not an arbitrary boundary line, given their altogether fundamental and therefore unparalleled meanings.

In geometric figures, space becomes form; in rhythm, time becomes number; the world is woven of figures and rhythms, whose beauty or ugliness lies respectively in their regularity or irregularity. And this shows that beauty does not pertain to form alone, but also to number, in the sense that perfect forms—especially the human body—comprise number in their structure; and it is number which, precisely, constitutes the regularity and hence the aesthetic value of these forms. And if every form is implicitly a number on the one hand, on the other every number is implicitly a form.

In the category of form, a figure of primary importance is the cross, which is the very symbol of symmetry both with respect to verticality and to horizontality. Vertically, symmetry expresses opposition; horizontally, it expresses complementarity. From another point of view, the vertical line represents creative projection or cosmogonic prolongation, or yet—and thereby— universal totality, the juxtaposition *Ātmā-Māyā*; the horizontal line, for its part, if it represents in the first place differentiations which are existentially equivalent although functionally unequal, it nonetheless comprises incompatibilities such as moral or aesthetic oppositions.[13] Strictly speaking, the vertical axis sets "degrees" into opposition—although the word "degree" risks being improper—such as absolute and relative, principle and manifestation, essential and formal, substantial and accidental, we might even say, *cum grano salis*, being and nothingness; whereas the horizontal axis sets "modes" into opposition, such as active and passive, dynamic

[13] Regarding geometrical symbols generally, let us add that "tri-dimensionality" makes the symbolism more complex by introducing into the horizontal plane the subjective and the objective, the initial and the terminal, in short, poles that refer to experience, transition, becoming.

and static, rigorous and gentle, *et cetera.* However, the modes are necessarily prefigured on the vertical axis, just as conversely the degrees are reflected on the horizontal axis; which in each case—*mutatis mutandis*—confers a new significance upon the elements under consideration. And the following is a principle of primary importance: each thing that we distinguish from the Sovereign Good either prolongs it or is opposed to it, at least apparently, for nothing can really be opposed to God.

Until now we have spoken of the four container-categories: object, subject, space, time; and the four content-categories: matter, energy, form, number; next come the attribute categories: quality, quantity, simplicity, complexity, which determine the modes of the preceding categories. Each of the latter comprises in fact one or more qualitative aspects, and then one or more quantitative aspects: an object may possess value because it is made of a precious material, but it may also possess it through the symbolism and beauty of its form; analogously, an object can be imposing either on account of its extent or by its repetition or multitude. Quality can be either substantial or "expressional"; and quantity can be either continuous or discontinuous.

The notion of "size" implied in that of quantity leads us to the following point. In all the existential categories there is an opposition between the "infinitely great" and the "infinitely small", according to the appropriate modes; now nothing can be metaphysically infinite outside the Absolute, hence we must acknowledge that the "two infinities", the small and the great—the word "infinite" having then but a relative and empirical meaning[14]—necessarily reach a limit, doubtless unimaginable, but nonetheless conceivable. For one can perfectly well conceive that both apparent infinitudes open onto nothingness in a certain sense, by a kind of supersaturation and "ontological explosion"—if one may express oneself thus—whose principle or prefiguration is given by the specific limitation itself of the categories.

[14] When we speak of the "infinite", we mean simply that which is without limits in its order; we see no reason to reserve this term for the metaphysical Infinite only, especially since the customs of language do not oblige us to do so.

Let us note in this connection that from the standpoint of human nature, the infinitely great and the infinitely small are in principle two abysses of exile and terror; we say in principle, because in fact it is scarcely possible to pierce the protective walls of our cosmic position—a position at once providential and normative, man being the real measure of things on pain of being deprived of sufficient reason. What we wish to stress here is that there are cosmic dimensions which by their nature are forbidden to man, mercifully in a certain sense; to attempt to cross our barriers is to forsake the human and thus the divine.[15] For it is starting from our providential cosmic position that we can and must realize the meaning of life, and understand deeply that "the kingdom of God is within you".

As regards the notions of "largeness" and "smallness", it may be objected that both of these characteristics represent eminently relative evaluations, and that nothing is small or large in itself—which is both true and false; false, because it amounts to forgetting firstly that the measures of things correspond to archetypal realities, hence to divine intentions, and secondly that man is a criterion of these intentions owing to the fact that his intelligence is "central" hence "total", which is precisely the reason for being of the human condition. In other words: a thing is great, extrinsically, because we are less great than it is and, intrinsically, in virtue of the existential possibility it manifests; human subjectivity here is not the cause of some optical illusion, but the consequence of realities, the adequate perception of which is foreseen by the Creator. This point is of extreme importance, for it supports the entire theory of symbolism; moreover, if all evaluation were merely relative or subjective, nothing would be left to evaluate, and the notions of quantity, quality, and primacy would lose all meaning. What has just been said shows the falseness of the evolutionist idea that man—his spirit as well as his form—is merely some phase among a thousand others, and thus that there is nothing quasi-absolute, perfect, or definitive in this phenomenon "made in the image of God"; in short, that instead of the projection of meaningful archetypes there is nothing but an altogether contingent chain of insignificant forms, always transitory and *ipso facto* monstrous.

[15] Nuclear physics and the "conquest of space" are enterprises of this kind, of which the least that can be said is that they are totally lacking in *barakah*.

But let us return after this digression to the general question of the attribute-categories, or more exactly to that of the two categories "simplicity" and "complexity". Each category comprises a kernel and an unfolding; we might also say: a "root" and a "crown". For space, for example, the root is quite obviously the point or the center, and the crown is the void or distance; for matter, the root is ether, and the crown, the five elements and the chemical substances; for form, the root is the sphere, and the crown, the multitude of figures and volumes.

It should be noted that there are perfect and imperfect forms, just as there are precious and vile materials, whereas such an alternative does not seem to exist either for space or time, as quality in them appears to reside in their general aspects rather than in some accident; yet space, which in itself has no center, is like a fabric woven of "stars", in other words, by its very nature it realizes the qualitative idea of the central point, of which sacred geography offers numerous examples, if only in a symbolic and approximate manner. And similarly, time by its very nature comprises "golden ages" which—aside from their necessary cyclical manifestations—are also reflected in a more or less contingent manner in the order of human phenomena. To speak of "space" is to speak of a "network"; to speak of "time" is to speak of "rhythm".

That which must be, hence that which cannot not be, is realized through the categories; they constitute the "theater" of all the modalities of the possible, modalities that are either plausible or paradoxical. In addition, it is important to distinguish between what is possible in principle and what is possible in fact—and likewise as regards impossibilities. In other words, it is necessary to distinguish between things which are realized because they must be so by their very nature, and those which could be realized but are prevented from being so by some contingent cause—and similarly, but conversely, for impossibilities, which may be either principial or accidental, and this to varying degrees. Moreover, it should be specified that there are two main orders of possibilities, the hypostatic and the cosmic, both orders containing possibilities which are either hierarchically arranged or else simply diverse; this is the *distinguo* between degrees and modes—or between the "vertical" and the "horizontal"—of which the cross is universally the symbol.

Previously, and parenthetically, we have considered the problem of good and evil; closely related to this question is that of being and nothingness, although the latter term does not represent any direct reality, while nevertheless comprising an indirect one, as is shown by the very existence of the word. Of course, being and nothingness—as well as good and evil—cannot be viewed as existential categories; however they are each a kind of prototype of them, as are the Absolute and the Infinite or, in a "vertical" sense,[16] Principle and Manifestation, *Ātmā* and *Māyā*. It might be objected here that nothingness, being nothing, cannot be the prototype of anything; this is precisely the question we would like to examine here as a matter of practical interest.

The notion of "nothing" is essentially a reference—obviously negative—to something possible or existent, otherwise it would be meaningless and even inconceivable. Indeed, "nothing" indicates by definition the absence of something: it excludes one or many objects or, depending on the context, all objects; to speak of an intrinsic "nothingness", of a nothing in itself, without reference to the things which it excludes, would be a contradiction in terms. When a receptacle is filled and then emptied, there is a difference; now this difference is a reality, otherwise no one would ever complain about being robbed. If this "nothing" were in itself a "nothingness"—if it had no "referential" character—there would be no difference between presence and absence, plenitude and vacuity, existence and inexistence; and every thief could argue that the "nothing" he produced in someone's purse does not exist; the word "nothing" would be devoid of meaning just as the nothingness is devoid of content. "Nothing", envisaged in a concrete context, can in actual fact compete with a "something"; while an intrinsic nothingness cannot concretely be opposed to anything or be affected by anything in any way. And similarly space, if it were an absolute emptiness—if it did not in actuality coincide with ether—could not comprise an element of distance and separation, for a nothingness added to another nothingness— if this were conceivable without absurdity—could not produce a distance.

[16] In order of superposition or hierarchy, not of juxtaposition or complementarity.

A logically utilizable "nothing" has therefore nothing absolute about it; it is by definition relative to something, although in a negative manner. However, it comprises an aspect of absoluteness through the totality of the negation it represents: the difference between 1 and 2 is relative, but the difference between 1 and 0 can be termed absolute, with evident metaphysical reservations. A thing cannot exist halfway, either it exists or it does not exist; consequently, since there is something absolute about existence in relation to non-existence—this being the whole miracle of creation—there is likewise *ipso facto* something absolute or total about the negation or exclusion of something existent—not the negation "in itself", but in relation to the absence of that which it negates or excludes; this is our well-known thesis of the "relatively absolute".[17]

The idea of "being" implies, positively, reality and, restrictively, manifestation; we say "restrictively" because manifestation or existence represents a less or a limitation in relation to the Principle which is pure Being. In signifying reality, the idea of "being" evokes *ipso facto* the "good" and also the "more", hence quality and quantity; but above all it evokes "presence". As for the opposite idea of "nothingness", it implies first of all the "absence" of being, or impossibility, and more relatively the absence of specific things; it also implies—by derivation and by analogy—the phenomenon of "less" and, in another respect, that of "evil". But this idea can also apply, quite paradoxically, to the transcendent or principial order: "nothingness", from the standpoint of the manifested world—hence from the standpoint of existence in the restricted sense of the term—is all that transcends this world and consequently is free from existential limitations.[18]

—— ·⁝· ——

When we examine the existential categories, it is certainly not to encourage an iconoclastic perspective aiming at "reducing" phenomena

[17] When one, two, or three out of four candles are extinguished, the difference in luminosity is relative; but when the last one is extinguished, the difference is total, for it is the difference between light and darkness.

[18] This is what allows one to apply to pure Being, and *a fortiori* to Beyond-Being, negative expressions such as "the Void" (*Shūnya*), "not this, not this" (*neti neti*), and other terms of the kind. All apophatic theology stems from this principle of terminology.

to their structural conditions, for it is the content, the message, the divine intention which has priority, and not the mechanism of the manifestation; however, this mechanism, when considered in itself, can in its turn signify a divine mystery, and that is precisely the case of the categories of which the world is woven. One has to insist on this: nothing is more aberrant than to cry victory because one believes one has deconstructed a beauty by reducing it to some mechanism or other, as if the sufficient reason for such a mechanism were not its result; but this is the very essence of the "demystification" so dear to modern man. The realistic attitude towards existence is fundamentally one of respect, not scorn; of worship, not impiety; of praise, not blasphemy. The supreme Being is not only the quasi-mathematical and structuring Principle of things, it is also—and even above all—the Sovereign Good which, as such, wishes to overflow in order to impart its values.

The primacy of the divine intention—hence of the message—in the domain of appearances, implies a highly paradoxical but nonetheless pertinent consequence, namely the existence of a "double reality" which makes one think of the "double truth" of the Scholastics. That is to say, in certain cases one has to distinguish between a "reality of fact" and a "reality of appearance": that the earth is round and turns around the sun is a fact, but that it is flat and that the sun travels from one horizon to another is, in the divine intention, no less a reality for us; otherwise the experience of man—a central and thus "omniscient" creature—would not be, *a priori* and "naturally", limited to these physically illusory but symbolically meaningful observations. And yet, from a certain point of view the physical illusion is relative, since for man the earth is unquestionably made up of flat regions, and only their sum—imperceptible to earthly creatures—constitutes a sphere, so much so that one should say that the earth is at once flat and round. As for traditional symbolism, it implies a moral consequence, which allows us to conclude that man is only entitled, in principle and *a priori*, to a knowledge that he can bear or that he is capable of assimilating; hence a knowledge that he can integrate into the total and spiritual knowledge which he is meant to possess in his quality as *homo sapiens*.[19]

[19] Unquestionably, modern science abounds in knowledge, but it is an established fact that man cannot bear it, either intellectually or morally. It is not for nothing that the sacred Scriptures tend to be as naive as possible; this provokes no doubt the mockery of skeptics, but it does not prevent either the simple or the wise from sleeping peacefully.

If the earth seems to be motionless while the heavens seem to turn around it, that is because manifestation is passive in relation to the Principle, which is active and determines it.[20] In a certain sense, the earth is us, and heaven is time to which we are subject; whence the relationship—not absolute, but nonetheless real—between the stars and our destiny.

—— ·:· ——

By the nature of things, each category is an image of God and therefore manifests a relationship according to which God may be envisaged. It will doubtless be objected that our categories are strictly existential, hence "creaturely", with the exception of the first two, namely object and subject. But such is not the case, for if it goes without saying that the space and time which we know and which determine us pertain to the world of our experience, it is no less obvious that they manifest truly universal conditions which *ipso facto* encompass all that exists, although according to very different modes resulting from All-Possibility; in other words, "to exist" is to be included in a "space" and a "time". As regards All-Possibility, or more precisely the "forms" that it actualizes or projects, we shall make the following observation: on the one hand, God always manifests the same principles, possibilities, or archetypes, because being absolute He is immutable, hence always identical to Himself; on the other hand, He manifests them in modes that are always new, from cycle to cycle, because being infinite He comprises inexhaustible possibilities.

It is easy to discover the prefiguration of the couple Matter-Energy *in divinis*: indeed, God is "Substance" and "Energy", "Being" and "Possibility"; which leads us to the *distinguo* between the Absolute and the Infinite, or more exactly between the Absoluteness and Infinitude of the Sovereign Good.

[20] A Muslim would say that if the immobility of the sun—in relation to the planets—is not visible to men, that is so they will not think that the sun is God. It should not be forgotten, moreover, that the sun, along with its entire planetary system, moves in its turn; which fact would have allowed Ptolemy—*mutatis mutandis*—to make his own Galileo's famous exclamation: *Eppur si muove!*

Let us now return to the complementarity Space-Time, but envisaged at the ontological level. God is, on the one hand, the "Infinite" and, on the other, the "Eternal"; but from another angle, if one were to say that God is "Space", it would mean that He is Possibility inasmuch as it contains, conserves, and diversifies; and if one were to say that He is "Time", it would mean that He is Possibility inasmuch as it produces, modifies, destroys, and causes succession. And if space has regions, time has cycles; however, "divine Regions" and "divine Cycles" are not intrinsic divine Qualities; they concern only the relationships between God and the world.

To speak of the divine "Form" is a contradiction in terms, unless by this word is meant the Perfection of the Sovereign Good, at the degree of Being and not beyond. Be that as it may, it is easy to conceive why the sun is an image of the divine Being: its form is perfect since it is spherical, its rays are innumerable and limitless; it is made of matter and energy and it produces both heat and light—all of which are symbols of the divine Archetype. It is true that from the angle of transcendence nothing resembles God—certain theologians insist upon this not without fierceness, notably Maimonides—whereas from the angle of immanence everything attests to God, if only by the sole miracle of existence. "Nothing is like unto Him", proclaims the Koran, but also: "God is the light of the heavens and of the earth", and "God's Hand is above their hands". It could also be said that every positive thing necessarily resembles God, but that He resembles nothing.[21]

Intrinsically, "quantity" refers to the unlimitedness of the divine Qualities, hence of the Names of God. As regards "God-Number", there is also a mathematical symbolism to consider: as we have remarked more than once—the question, moreover, admits of no doubt—one may conceive, in the divine Order, a Duality, a Trinity, a Quaternity; but the number is then Pythagorean and no longer has any relationship to quantity; it becomes on the contrary qualitative and coincides, by analogy, with geometric forms. In fact, this is intrinsic number—represented arithmetically by the divisions of unity—whereas number in the ordinary sense of the word is extrinsic, hence quantitative.[22]

[21] One could, however, qualify every religion as being a "divine Form"; and all the more so the "hypostatic Face" which is revealed in each religion and which characterizes it.

[22] The fundamental geometric figures—point, circle, square, cross, spiral—can signify "divine Forms" in the sense that each of them from a certain angle retraces the rela-

The universal poles are the object and the subject. As "Object", God is Reality, the only one that is; now Reality coincides with the knowable: only that is knowable which is real, and conversely. As "Subject", God is Consciousness, again the only one that is; this Consciousness coincides with its content, the sole Real. Relativity is the bipolarization into subject and object; hence into "point of view" and "aspect".

Thus the question of knowing whether "everything began" with the subject or with the object is altogether vain; each of the two poles can be interpreted as the absolute origin of the world. Doubtless one may distinguish between a metaphysics that is "existential" as regards its starting-point, and another that is "intellectual", in the same respect;[23] but on condition of adding that the pole chosen contains the other pole, and that there is thus only a difference of accentuation involved in the choice, and not an exclusive principle. All told, the metaphysician needs both perspectives: the "objectivist" vision being determined primarily by the discernment of the Principle inasmuch as it manifests the Universe, and the "subjectivist" vision on the contrary having in view above all the reintegration—at some level—of consciousness into its Archetype, the divine Self. At some level: for "in my Father's house are many mansions".

We have said above that every category comprises a root; now this root is a kind of theophany or sacrament. Thus the spiritual significance of these roots or seeds is plain to see: the category "object", whose point of departure is "the other" in itself, requires on our part discernment, the sense of the real, attachment to the truth, justice—hence also humility; and the category "subject", whose point of departure is the most intimate "oneself", namely the "heart", requires contemplation, the sense of the sacred, inwardness, holiness—hence also charity. Space evokes, still from the standpoint of spiritual alchemy, the mystery of the center, which coincides with that of the heart-intellect; time evokes the mystery of the present, which coincides with that of

tionship between the Absolute and the Relative, *Ātmā* and *Māyā*, or *Nitya* and *Līlā*; and this *in divinis* as well as in the manifested Universe.

[23] It is thus that *Vedānta* is founded on the subjective symbolism of the "Self". And in Sufism, there is the quasi-rivalry between a school founded upon "Being" (*Wujūd*) and another founded upon "Perception" (*Shuhūd*).

spiritual wakefulness. Infinite center and eternal present, the purified heart is Elijah's altar upon which the heavenly fire descends.

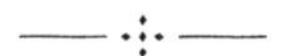

The overview of the existential categories is important because it pertains not only to knowledge of the world, but also to the knowledge of God: the categories are hypostases which are prolonged in creation and govern it. They are "divinities"—or archangelic projections—which in the final analysis become manifest before our very eyes and within our very being, and which constitute the warp and weft of existence or of the universe. Of all this profane man has no awareness; with the assurance of a sleepwalker, he moves exclusively in the fragile contents of the cosmic fabric, the divine workmanship of which he practically forgets, whence an unrealistic overestimation of things and facts as well as of himself—as if phenomena were absolute and as if earthly life were eternal. In this there lies a prodigious lack of imagination, all the more astonishing and absurd in that it affects men who are supposed to be intelligent and who hold to being so, but who precisely forget that intelligence is the perception of the real and not the "intellectualization" of the unreal.

A priori, man is indeed obliged to register concrete phenomena and this is quite normal for him, all the more so in that phenomena can be meaningful, to say the least, and that there are phenomena which are sacred; but while looking at phenomena with the respect that may be due them, man must be deeply aware of that universal and underlying mystery which is the manifestation of *Ātmā*. And this awareness not only prolongs necessarily the awareness we have of the Absolute as such, but also confers upon our relationship with phenomena its rightful proportions, its legitimacy, its nobility, and its spiritual significance.

2. Concerning an Onto-Cosmological Ambiguity

When the Intellect envisages the divine Reality from the standpoint of the Absolute, this Reality reveals itself as perfectly one, or "non-dual"—as the Vedantists would say in order to avoid any suspicion of limiting determination; but when this same Reality is envisaged by the Intellect starting from the Relative, it reveals itself under the three hierarchized aspects of Principle-Essence, Principle-Person, and Principle-Demiurge. The word "Principle" is repeated here intentionally, in order to show clearly that it is always a question of the one and indivisible Reality.

The importance of these distinctions appears concretely when one speaks of God's "will" and His "actions"; in so doing one readily reduces divine Reality to the Person alone, while improperly claiming for the latter the metaphysical prerogatives of the Essence along with the cosmic activities of the Demiurge. This is the common perspective of the anthropomorphic monotheism of the Semites; and since this way of looking at things gives rise to inevitable contradictions, the theologies—and even the Scriptures in their own way—speak of mysteries and in response to our need for logical explanations opt to beg the question. If we come back here to a problem which we have dealt with more than once, it is with the intention of clarifying the problem of divine causality—*ad majorem Dei gloriam*—and of situating the principle of evil, the existence of which is one of the great pitfalls of religious thinking.

Possibility as such, that is to say universal Possibility, belongs to the Principle-Essence; the Principle-Person, for its part, is not responsible for Possibility, because it merely crystallizes the fundamental consequences thereof, namely the archetypes or the "ideas". The Principle-Demiurge, in its turn, does not bear the responsibility for the archetypes; it merely transfers them to the universal substance, whose center it occupies; and this obliges it to differentiate and particularize them, as well as to contrast them, in conformity with the characteristic structure of this substance.

In other words: Possibility as such pertains to the supreme and essential Principle; the fundamental possibilities, for their part, originate in the self-determined and personal Principle; whereas the contingent possibilities are ascribable to the manifested and demiurgic Principle, even down to the most insignificant "chance happenings", which are nonetheless "willed by God" since they exist. And it is from this third "hypostasis" of the Principle that the evil genius derives, not directly, but by a sort of "fall", ontologically foreseen since a radiation always implies a movement away from the Center.

In Semitic monotheism, Satan appears first of all as an evil genius paradoxically in the service of God:[1] he is at one and the same time the accuser, the seducer, and the corrupter; it is only later that he reveals himself as the enemy of God and as the principle of evil itself. In the Koran as in the Bible, the *princeps huius mundi* manifests himself under the two aspects just mentioned: he is the vehicle for carrying out such and such a punishment willed by God as well as for his own revolt against all divine volition. Indeed, the Bible sometimes attributes ways of acting to God that it could with better reason attribute to the adversary: when God "hardens the heart of Pharaoh", He necessarily does so in an indirect manner and by means of the cosmic power of subversion; thus it is that Islamic theology specifies that "God leads into error"—according to the Koran—by turning away from man, not by determining him, which amounts to saying that God "permits" evil but does not accomplish it. "Turning away" from man, God abandons him to the devil whom man himself had chosen previously; and that is why the Koran says more than once that it is not God who wrongs man but that it is man who wrongs himself; metaphysically, man punishes or condemns himself *a priori* by his initial and substantial possibility.[2] It should be pointed out here that the "devil"

[1] The *Midrash*, and after it the Koran, attribute the same paradox to Solomon, who had in his service demons to carry out all sorts of tasks; something which is indirectly connected with magic, accessible *de jure* to initiates only. Another example of this same paradox, in human society, is the executioner, the "legalized criminal" who executes the judge's sentences.

[2] This is the meaning of the "primordial pact" between God and man: "And when thy Lord brought forth their descendants from the loins of the sons of Adam and took them to witness against themselves, saying, Am I not your Lord? They answered, Yea, we do bear witness. This was done lest ye should say, at the day of Resurrection:

is less the principle of evil than the adaptation of this principle to the human world, hence the personification of the genius of darkness; in which case, he pertains, not to the principial order, but to the psychic domain. He is "made of fire", as the Koran says, and he is a *jinn*, not a principial power, although he prolongs the latter; but this prolongation amounts, precisely, to a sort of fall.

If for the shamanists there is no devil, that is because they envisage evil in its principial and non-humanized aspect; they distinguish between a "divinity" who is beneficent and another who is maleficent, because all the cosmic laws have a celestial origin. Although man necessarily occupies a central position in the Universe, he does not detach himself from it nor does he oppose it; shamanism is not "humanistic" and for that reason man does not appear as the lord, or even the tyrant, of the surrounding world; a personification of evil is scarcely called for in a world where man is organically integrated into a more or less divine whole. We meet with this perspective likewise in Hinduism, where evil is deified as well as "demonized"; it is well known that Hinduism tends to realize every possible perspective, from monotheism to shamanism. For that matter, even the Koran makes Job say, "the devil hath afflicted me with calamity and pain" (*Sūrah* "*Sad*" [38]:41), whereas, according to the Islamic perspective—or the monotheistic perspective in general—illnesses like all other trials in life could only come from a divine will; *mā shāʾa ʾLlāh*; in the aforementioned passage there is thus a projection of a divine function into the demon, or on the contrary a "demonization" of the same *a priori* divine, but privative, function. Likewise, in Shiva—not the supreme Shiva of course, which is identical with *Para-brahma*, but the demiurgic Shiva of the *Trimūrti*—it is not always easy to make a clear separation between principial necessity and demoniacal initiative; or between the wrath of Heaven and this or that malefic caprice of the *samsāra*.[3]

Verily, of this were we unaware" (Koran, *Sūrah* "The Heights" [7]:172). This means that the particular individual possibility contains by definition the consciousness of the divine and normative Possibility, to which it conforms or to which it is opposed; the opposition being the "luciferian" desire to be "like God".

[3] Goethe's Mephisto confuses the two things: for him, evil is "sin and destruction"; sin pertains, however, to Satan, and destruction to Shiva. Satan causes souls to lose themselves, smiling; Shiva causes their salvation, fulminating. In principle, one could admit that death comes from the devil since he is the one who is primarily responsible for it,

Be that as it may, there is some ambiguity, traditionally speaking, concerning certain negative functions of the Logos-Demiurge on the one hand, and particular aspects of satanic personification on the other, so much so that one could say that the lowest point of the demiurgic domain and the highest point of the satanic domain can coincide, as is shown by certain terrifying images of divinities, in the Mahayanic as well as in the Hindu pantheon. For "it takes all kinds to make a world"; even a celestial one.

The myth of Lucifer's fall—or the "fall of the angels"—can be interpreted at different levels, but the most profound meaning is the one which pertains to the ontological order. The realm of *Māyā*—the total Universe—extends starting from God the Creator inclusively all the way to what we would call "nothingness" if it existed; the reason we can speak of it, is that nothingness exists as a tendency, let us say, or under the appearance of a power, ungraspable in itself, which eats away at existing things: things being within its reach by the fact that they are situated in the "peripheral" or "terrestrial" world, the *samsāra*—not in the "central" and "celestial" world, the *Svarga.* Thus, the whole Universe is situated between two "voids", one divine and concrete, and one cosmic and abstract: the Principle-Essence, which is above Being itself, and the nothing which, placed evidently "beneath" existence, tends to negate and to pervert the latter. This is all that divine Possibility concedes to impossibility, and it does so while lending impossibility a semblance of indirect reality—by virtue of the Infinitude from which All-Possibility derives; or rather, with which it coincides.

Thus, what is the highest affirms itself also at the lowest rung of the ladder; that is what the seal of Solomon symbolizes. Nothingness pure and simple seems to be opposed to the divine Nought, for the principial Reality always appears as a nothingness in relation to

given the fact that he caused the fall of man and the loss of Paradise; but *de facto*, death is attributed to God's will, or more directly—in Islam—to the intervention of the Archangel Izrail, described as being the "most terrible" being that God created, and comparable, therefore, to the black and terrifying goddess Kali, the spouse of Shiva.

the inferior degrees;[4] we say "seems", because nothing can oppose the Absolute. When a tree is reflected in a lake, its summit is at the bottom in the reflected image; this is what happens also, or rather *a priori*, in the ontological order. The reflected and inverted summit of the tree is unreal—since it is only an optical illusion—like nothingness that intends, by annihilating the world, to transcend it, and thus tends to imitate—or to "ape"—the Transcendence of the supreme Principle.

Let us summarize: the realm of *Māyā*—which extends from the personal and creating God to the material world—is as if suspended between two voids: the "divine Nought", which we term thus because there is not a trace of determination or affirmation in it; and nothingness properly speaking—nothingness pure and simple—about which one can speak only on account of its existential effects: it is the "existing inexistence" or the "possible impossibility". The All and the nothing: the All is so overflowing that it even lends an appearance of existence to nothingness.[5] Some people might ask: Why is this so? One could just as well ask why Being is Being; it is the very nature of Being which provides the answer.

—— ·:· ——

The All or the nothing, we have said. That is also the profound meaning of Zoroastrian dualism: Ahuramazda or Ormuzd is "That which alone is", and Angra Mainyu or Ahriman, "that which is not" but "wishes to be" to the detriment of that which is; it is always the illusory struggle—in *Māyā*—of the impossible against All-Possibility. But where then, one may ask, will this impossible, or this nothingness travestied transitorily as something possible, be at the final victory of Ormuzd? First of all, one must not confuse the laws of cosmic cycles—not even the great universal cycle—with the laws of ontology,

[4] The creator God likewise appears as a void from the human standpoint, whence the "obscure merit of faith"; whence too the possibility of atheism, for those who believe only in what they see.

[5] From the standpoint of human intelligibility, *Māyā* is a greater mystery than *Ātmā*; and within the framework of *Māyā*, evil is a greater mystery than the good. Within the framework of evil finally, human absurdity is a greater mystery, if one may say so, than natural calamities.

which coincide with pure principles; from the standpoint of these principles, the victory is always there since the Principle alone is real: the "supreme Nought" precisely. As for the cosmic cycles, the final victory means, not that the possibility of operatively satanic "nothingness" is abolished, but that the door of existence is closed to it; "efficient nothingness", so to speak, is always included in All-Possibility as a potentiality, and this, let it be said again, in virtue of the Infinitude of the "divine Nought". Infinity implies by definition the at least symbolical possibility of its own negation; whence the "existentialization" of nothingness. "And the more man blasphemes", Meister Eckhart says, "the more he praises God"; in puffing itself up with pride in order to deny That which is, "existentialized" nothingness pays homage to Being, the source of all existence.

III.
SPIRITUAL PERSPECTIVES

1. Degrees and Dimensions of Theism

Each of the ideas associated with the term "theism" can have a legitimate meaning, on condition that it be interpreted according to a metaphysically correct intention. Even "atheism" has an admissible meaning if—when interpreted according to the Buddhist point of view—it refers to an exclusively "subjective" and immanentist perspective, and this in a spiritual, not humanistic and profane, sense of course. However, this term is too spoiled by its purely negative application to be acceptable in any plausible way. Similarly, all the other expressions constructed with "theism" are somewhat hazardous because of their conventional use, except for the word "monotheism"; but our purpose here is not to explain terms, but things; we shall use terms simply as points of reference.

Having voiced these reservations, we could call "metatheism" the Vedantic or Taoist idea of a supra-ontological Reality—the supra-personal *Ātmā*—in order to indicate clearly that this idea basically transcends all theism properly so called; for a "God" creates, speaks, legislates, judges, and saves, which the divine Essence could not do, since by definition it excludes all *Māyā*, and consequently has no associate. Doubtless, theism—or monotheism—does not negate this Essence, but it leaves it aside, taking it into account only incidentally and timidly—except in the case of esoterism or the highest mysticism—or by ascribing it to the personal God; this is the origin of the contradictions between a Sovereign Good which, while being necessarily opposed to evil and while being omnipotent, seems nonetheless to "will" evil since it does not prevent it. We shall not return here to the solution of this paradox, which we have dealt with in the two preceding chapters and on other occasions.

After theism properly so called, which is based upon the distinction between the creative Principle and the created world, it is necessary to consider what may be termed "pneumatotheism" or "uranotheism", the first expression referring to the "Spirit of God" which is reflected at the center of the cosmos, and the second referring to the "Heavens" which God inhabits, according to the Lord's Prayer. Even monotheism, rigorous as it is in its distinction between God and the world, Creator and created, Principle and manifestation, includes "divine Manifestation" in an incidental manner within the principial Order, exactly as it sometimes includes—in an inverse sense[1]—the Essence in the Person, to the extent, precisely, that it cannot help being conscious of the Essence or of its traces.

But monotheism will never go so far as to include in the divine Order the infra-angelic world of the "spirits", that is, psychic creatures; thus it will never accept what may be designated by the term "pantheism". We use this term here without lending it the deist and Spinozan meaning that it has conventionally,[2] for the Divinity-synthesis in question is not the *Deus sive natura* of the philosophers. Indeed, for the shamanists—who are the traditional "pantheists"— God is situated above the world, but He penetrates it and manifests Himself "consciously" through the angels and the spirits;[3] this is the religion of the Siberians, of Bön-Po Tibetans, the Shintoists, the American Indians, and even, as regards its mythological foundation, the Confucianists and the Taoists. It is easy to conceive how this "pantheism" is linked to magic if one takes into account the practically divine function assumed in it by the "spirits", namely, the *kami* of Shintoism and the *manitu* or *wakan* of the Indian tradition of North America.

The above represents the extreme limit of what still may be properly termed "theism"; what lies below is pantheism in the classical sense of the word, for which God is all that exists, no more no less. It may perhaps be objected that for the shamanists also, each animal and each plant is a divine manifestation; but in this case, it is the underlying soul that counts, or the genius of the species, hence the archetype, and not the physical form as such. The metaphysician, who is not thereby a shamanist, nonetheless shares in this way of looking at things: for him, everything is integrated into the universal Substance, hence into Existence, and then into given Qualities, Faculties, or Functions, for "everything is *Ātmā*"; but this outlook never constitutes the total doc-

[1] That is, in this case the "annexation" operates in a descending direction, whereas in the preceding case it operates in an ascending direction. Be that as it may, it would be improper to take the word "God" exclusively in the usual and personalist sense, unless the context demands this restriction.

[2] The term "pantheism" originated with an English "free thinker" of the eighteenth century, John Toland, whose aim was to deny anything supernatural in religion.

[3] Such as sylphs, salamanders, undines, gnomes. Paracelsus discussed these kinds of creatures; they are the elves of the Scandinavians and the *jinn* of the Arabs. Fairies and peris, feminine genii, belong to the same category.

trine, it is simply an aspect of what we have termed the "metatheistic" perspective. For "extremes meet": to understand the divine Essence is at the same stroke to understand the "indirect divinity" of all that is "not nothing"; but this understanding has no connection with an exclusive, hence abusive, worship of spirits or visible phenomena. An authentic metaphysician spontaneously feels a certain respect for natural phenomena inasmuch as they manifest universal Possibility, and which for that reason bear the signature of the Absolute.[4]

To return to the question of pantheism, we would say that it is essentially the point of view of immanence; now immanence is not only the presence of the divine in our soul, it is also this presence around us, in the world—just as inversely, transcendence is the inaccessibility of God, not only above us, in the heavens, but also within us, in the depths of the heart.[5] There are two deviations of immanentism, one objective and the other subjective: the first is either idolatry or the idolatrous worship of the phenomena of nature; the second is the self-divinization of a monarch, notably that of the Biblical Pharaoh, and later that of the Roman emperors.

—— ·:· ——

So many theisms, so many forms of worship: "logolatry"—the worship of the *Avatāra*—corresponds to "pneumatotheism" or "uranotheism", which we may also term "logotheism"; and the worship (if this word is still applicable here) of the immanent Logos, namely of the pure Intellect, is also related metaphysically to the worship of the *Avatāra*. "Heliolatry", or "astrolatry" in general, is related to pantheism, as is also, in many cases, "zoolatry", but through deviation clearly, if by "latry" we mean an adoration properly so called.

[4] Hinduism being a tradition based upon metaphysics, the pantheistic perspective is necessarily manifested within it, as is shown by such forms of worship as that of the sun, of the Ganges, and other phenomena of nature; without forgetting the worship of certain animals, such as the cow, for instance, or more precisely, the zebu, which was already sacred for the ancient Mesopotamians, and whose head, with its horns in the form of a crescent, recalls that of the Egyptian Apis.

[5] At least *a priori*, leaving out of consideration mystical union or metaphysical realization.

Regarding the worship of animals, the following has to be taken into account. Doubtless, animals are inferior to man, but with respect to the symbolism concerning spiritual realities, they can evoke principles, norms, ideals, and therefore also angelic powers, depending on the animal species in view—at least such is the case when the symbolism resides in the nature of the animal, not when it is conventionally added to it in virtue of a mere association of ideas, as is the case when the bear is seen as a symbol of royal power, and complementarily, the boar as a symbol of spiritual authority; in such cases, the symbolism is based, not on the intrinsic character of the animal, but upon an altogether outward aspect such as a particular physical detail or manner of behavior. Man is a central, hence integral or total being; he can be anything, depending on his individual quality or lack of quality; an animal, on the contrary, depending on the species, embodies either a particular quality or a particular lack of quality; in the first case, it is for man the living image of an archetype, a norm, an ideal, and can even become the vehicle or support of spiritual influences, so much so that the notion of "sacred animal" is not an empty word. That an animal can also become the vehicle of any kind of magical or psychic influences, explains its ambiguity, and thus the ambiguity of its worship; the uncertainty about its quality results from the half-heavenly half-earthly, or half-spiritual half-psychic nature of operative pantheism, hence of shamanism.[6]

Furthermore, one can distinguish even within one and the same theism several forms of worship: Islam, for example, offers us not only an adoration founded on the love of God—in virtue of the divine quality of "Benevolence" (*Rahmah*)[7]—but also an adoration founded

[6] Thus it is probable, in the case of the shamanism of the American Indians, that the proximity of Christianity, so harmful in some altogether extrinsic, accidental, and human respects, had at the same time an equilibrating influence from a strictly spiritual point of view, hence in virtue of the intrinsic values of the Christian message. Missionaries are one thing, and the Gospel is another.

[7] The term *Rahmah* also contains the ideas of Mercy and Beauty, and then those of Love, and coincides in the final analysis with the *Ānanda* of Brahmanism, radiant "Beatitude".

upon fear and the worship of Power; this second perspective—which is that of Ashari and, with some extenuating shades of meaning, that of Ghazzali—is in principle fundamental for Islamic theology, but in fact it is compensated in the collective consciousness by an attitude, if not of mystical love, at least of trust, and by other factors conforming to the needs and rights of human nature. Be that as it may, the great pitfall of monotheism is its need—since "God is one" and since this "One" is creative Being—to attribute to God on the one hand All-Possibility, which in reality pertains to Beyond-Being and for which the personal God could not be held responsible, and on the other hand the most contingent particular possibilities, which pertain to the Logos, center of the Universe and for that reason already "manifested" or cosmic.[8]

Let us not fear to make this last point more precise, at the risk of repeating ourselves, but with a concern for perfect clarity: there is something singularly disproportionate and implausible in imagining that the Sovereign Good could desire and predestine some particular trivial or vile event, as is assumed explicitly or implicitly by theologians anxious to safeguard at all cost the unity of a God at once absolute and personal. In reality, the personal God—a hypostasis already involved in Relativity although nonetheless situated beyond particular contingencies—could never "will" such and such "accidental" possibilities; rather, He affirms archetypal possibilities, so that it could be said that God wills possibilities "as such" without concerning Himself directly with "such and such possibilities".[9] Beyond-Being, or the supra-personal Essence, can only will All-Possibility in itself, which coincides with its tendency to radiate—this being the effect of its Infinitude.

[8] So as not to risk appearing to introduce a duality, let alone a plurality, into the one and personal God, the Semitic texts and their commentators beg the question by stating that God, being "all-powerful", "doeth what He will"; we find this argument in Isaiah, Job, and Saint Paul, as well as in the Koran. It is a double-edged argument, yet for certain psychological reasons it was efficacious for three or four millennia, in the climate for which it was destined.

[9] "Such and such possibilities": particular facts, determined by contingency. "Possibilities as such": the principial possibilities or archetypes. It is evident that one could also speak of "such and such principial possibilities" and of contingent possibilities "as such", but these are not in question here.

For example, the possibility of man—together with the creatures surrounding him and of which he is the summit and center—falling into this relatively inferior substance which is matter, whereas the substance really proportioned to living beings had been incorruptible and paradisal, is a possibility which could not but be realized, for reasons connected with the principle of universal expansion; now it is this principial possibility that is contained in the consciousness of Being, and not all the possibilities resulting from the "fall" and the multiple consequences and contingencies which it engendered; these come from the Logos only. It is in fact the Logos which directly rules the world, and thus it coincides with the Demiurge of Plato and of the Gnostics—and no less with the Hindu Trinity of the efficient Gods, Brahmā, Vishnu, and Shiva.[10]

But this is of key importance, when considering the risks of "pneumatotheism" and "angelolatry": Divinity, which is at once "Being" and "Consciousness",[11] comprises—in the direction of Relativity—different "strata of Knowledge", if one may so put it; but this does not prevent it from being absolutely one in itself, for the relationships differ depending on the perspectives. In none of its hypostatic self-determinations does it cease to be itself; it could not lose its simplicity, and it never ceases to be God. Clearly, a God who is mathematically "one" in every respect[12] could not produce existence; it is not conceivable how He could create the world and speak to man.

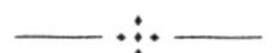

The Hindu spirit, with the penetration and suppleness characterizing it, takes perfectly into account the *distinguos* which we have just mentioned, but at the cost of what is rightly or wrongly termed "polytheism": wrongly, if by it one means that the supreme Principle is conceived as multiple, and rightly if one has in mind the more or

[10] And also—according to an obviously different perspective—with the four efficient "Archangels" of Islam, who pertain to *Rūh*, the "Divine Spirit".

[11] Or "Object" and "Subject".

[12] As Maimonides imagines, losing sight of the fact that it is not inasmuch as He is Absolute that God deals with the relative—the divine capacity of projection into relativity, or on the contrary of anticipating it, being an aspect of the divine Infinitude.

less popular forms of worship, without forgetting the mythological symbolisms by which they are inspired.

Hinduism, whose genius consists in excluding nothing, also comprises that very particular mode of religion which is "gynecolatry", not only because it admits of goddesses, but also and even above all because it practices, in one of its sectors, a monotheism in feminine mode.[13] Let us specify that the basis of all "gynecotheism" is the deiformity of the human being: if man is "made in the image of God", it is because God is in His way the transcendent prototype of man; now to speak of man, is also to speak of woman, since the human being comprises two sexes and since, quite obviously, woman is no less human than her masculine partner. Religious anthropomorphism gives rise to two perspectives: either one starts from the idea that man—the male—represents "totality" and thus includes woman, who is a "part"—since Biblically-speaking, Adam was before Eve—in which case Divinity is conceived in a masculine aspect, but not necessarily in an ostentatious manner; or else one starts from the idea that woman is "mother", hence "creatrix", and that moreover—or rather *a priori*—she manifests the Non-formal, the Infinite, the Mystery, in which case Divinity is conceived in a feminine aspect, or let us say, rather in its aspect of femininity. This second perspective is that of Shaktism; as for the first—"androtheism"—it is that of the three Semitic religions, with a certain exception in the case of Christianity which, without granting the Blessed Virgin the worship of "latria", does grant her, and to her alone, the worship of "hyperdulia", which practically, in spite of everything, amounts to a kind of divinization, if not "by right" at least "in fact."[14] In Hindu terminology, we would say that Mary is a feminine *Avatāra* of supreme degree, as is proven by her qualities of "Bride of the Holy Ghost" and "Co-Redemptress", not to mention the epithet—problematical as it is—of "Mother of God"; and as is also shown by the practice of the *Ave Maria*, which derives

[13] This form of worship—Shaktism—is most often situated within Shaivism. The one and supreme Goddess is Durga, the wife of Shiva; however, Shiva becomes secondary next to the all-powerful and omniscient *Shakti*, rather as is the case when the male and female principles are compared respectively to the moon and the sun, in keeping with the mysticism of dilating extinction in the "Eternal Feminine".

[14] Except in Protestantism which, in this respect, returns to the perspective of the Old Testament.

from the worship of the Logos, and consequently from the cosmic prolongation of the divine Order.

But all these distinctions between boundaries are not solely a question of doctrinal perspective, they are also a matter of religious sensibility, and on this plane we shall not argue whether a given option is well-founded or on the contrary insufficient; for if on the one hand man chooses his God, on the other hand too, God chooses his man.

2. "Our Father Who Art in Heaven"

In the monotheistic Semitic world, Christ was the only one to call God "my Father". Doubtless he was not the first to use this symbolism of paternity, examples of which we find in fact in the *Torah*: "I (*Yahweh*) will be his father, and he shall be my son" (2 Sam. 7:14); "Like as a father pitieth his children, so the Lord pitieth them that fear him" (Ps. 103:13); "thou, O Lord art our father" (Isa. 63:16); "But now, O Lord, thou art our father; we are the clay, and thou our potter; and we all are the work of thy hand" (Isa. 64:8); "for I (*Yahweh*) am a father to Israel, and Ephraim is my firstborn" (Jer. 31:9); "Have we not all one father? hath not one God created us?" (Mal. 2:10).

All this according to the *Torah*;[1] Christ, however, made of this symbolism a central idea —the very Name of God, so to speak. In calling God "Father", Christ attests to the "Sovereign Good": he refers on the one hand to the essentiality of the divine Goodness,[2] and on the other hand to the reciprocity between the Creator and the creature "made in His image"; this means that Christ grants priority, not to the divine Power and to the aspect of Lordship, but to the divine Love and to the aspect of Paternity, precisely; as a result, man presents himself, not as a simple slave, but as a child who, in relation to his Father, has the rights granted to him by that Father, and which stem from his being a "valid interlocutor" and "image of God".

In Christ's language, there is clearly a distinction to be made between "our Father" and "my Father": the relation of filiation is principial and potential in the former case, and fully actual and effective in the second. The ordinary man is "child of God" in the respect we have just indicated, that is, by the simple fact that he is man and hence "interlocutor"; but Christ is "child" or "son of God" in still another respect, which is superimposed onto the preceding; or it is,

[1] The expression "Our Father" is also to be found in the *Talmud* and in Jewish liturgy; in the latter it is used ten times a year and in connection with the expression "Our King".

[2] "Verily, my Mercy precedeth my Wrath", according to a *hadīth*; this indicates that Goodness pertains to the Essence. And similarly, according to the Koran: "Your Lord hath prescribed for Himself Mercy" (*Sūrah* "Cattle" [6]:54).

geometrically speaking, what the vertical dimension is to the horizontal, or what the sphere is to the circle: he is "child" or "son" by his personality and not by the simple fact that he belongs to the human species, nor by virtue of an initiation or a spiritual orientation capable of actualizing a potentiality of *theosis*. For the *Avatāra* is a cosmic phenomenon implying by definition every spiritual perfection possible—as well as every physical perfection—but which no realization on the part of an ordinary man could produce; the *yogin*, the *sannyāsin*, the *jnānin*, can realize *Brahma*, but he will never be Rama or Krishna.

At this point we would like to digress and say the following: on the one hand, the Gospel says of the Holy Virgin that she is "full of grace" and that "the Lord is with thee", and that "henceforth all generations shall call me blessed";[3] on the other hand, Christ inherited from the Virgin his entire human nature, from the psychic as well as physical point of view, so that his sacramental body and blood are fundamentally those of the Virgin. Now a person who possesses such prerogatives—to the point of being called "Mother of God"—necessarily has an "avataric" character, expressed theologically by the idea of "Immaculate Conception"; thus the cult of Mary is not merely a matter of tradition, it clearly results from Scripture.[4]

Theology is right to acknowledge that in Jesus there is a human nature and a divine nature and that in a certain respect both natures are united in a single person, that of Christ. However the distinction between a "nature"—human or divine, having its own will while not being a person—and a "person"—unique and indivisible, having two incommensurable and in principle divergent wills—this distinction greatly risks being reduced in the final analysis to a question of terminology. Be that as it may, we have no difficulty in acknowledging that the pitfalls implied in the definition of the God-man are beyond the resources of a thought that intends to avoid every misunderstanding

[3] The Koran says of Mary: "Verily God hath chosen thee and hath purified thee, and hath chosen thee above all the women of the world" (*Sūrah* "The Family of Imran" [3]:42).

[4] Protestantism knows nothing of this cult because its aim is to concentrate solely on the Christ-Savior, and because it minimizes the import of the passages that we have quoted, by referring to other passages apparently less favorable to Mary. The *upāya*, the "saving means", does not always conform to historical facts—very far from it—as is amply proven by many religious divergences.

at every level; and the same observation applies to certain implicit "clauses"—no doubt unusable dogmatically—in trinitarian theology.

—— ·⁝· ——

Unquestionably, the Christian notion of "child of God" indicates an element of esoterism which asserts itself, not in relation to all exoterism, since the notion itself also comprises an exoteric application, but—from the Christian point of view—in relation to the "Old Law" which seems to be formalistic and to some extent social rather than intrinsically moral. This is to say that the "New Law" represents in its own fashion the perspective of "inwardness" which transcends the perspective of formal prescriptions and observances, while imposing on man an esoterically practicable but socially unrealistic ascesis. Leaving aside the natural prerogatives of human deiformity, it could be said that it is by the spiritual attitude of inwardness or of essentiality that the "servant" of the "Lord" becomes effectively the "child" of the "Father", which, as a human being, he was potentially or virtually.

Let us specify the following points: the dietary prescriptions or the prohibitions concerning the Sabbath are plainly outward rules; by their very nature and quantity they constitute an "objective formalism"—willed by God in view of certain temperaments—but not necessarily a "subjective formalism", the latter being more or less a reduction of the religion to these observances. Be that as it may, the supreme Commandment—in Israel as everywhere else—is the love of God; this love may require that we be always aware of the profound and underlying reasons for given prescriptions, just as it may require only zeal in obedience to the Law; but neither our comprehension nor our zeal confers a quality of inwardness to the prescriptions themselves which by their nature are external. Thus esoterism, above all in the Hindu world, is fully conscious of the relative and conditional character of the rules of conduct; to deny this character is "subjective formalism", precisely.[5]

[5] A practice may be termed "formalistic" not because it is based upon a form—otherwise every spiritual practice would pertain to formalism—but because its immediate object belongs to the outward—hence *a priori* formal—order.

The Jew is child of God on account of the Election of Israel; the Christian is such on account of the Redemption. The Jew feels he is a child of God with respect to the "pagans", whereas the Christian feels that way even with regard to the Jews, whose perspective seems to him "exterior", or even "carnal". As for Islam, it does not have the notion of "Father" nor therefore that of "child", but it does have that of "Friend" (*Walī*), which is applied both to God and to man: to God who "lends assistance" and to the saints who "help" God; but Islam does not for all that give up the notion of "slave" since for Islam this notion is equivalent to that of "creature". Besides, the primacy accorded to the idea of "Lord"—and the complementary idea of "servant"—also has its merits, by the nature of things; its result is a profound resignation to the "Will of God", a resignation that refuses to ask God why He permits a given trial or does not grant a given favor, and that wisely combines the need for logical explanations with the sense of proportions.[6]

"Our Father who art in heaven": the specification "in heaven" indicates transcendence in relation to the earthly state, considered first from the objective and macrocosmic standpoint and then from the subjective and microcosmic standpoint. Indeed, "earth" or the "world" can be our individual and more or less sensorial soul as well as the ambience in which we live and which determines us, just as "heaven" can be our spiritual virtualities as well as the paradisiacal worlds; for "the kingdom of God is within you".

"Hallowed be Thy Name": this verb "to hallow" is almost synonymous with "to worship" and consequently with "to pray" or "to invoke". To worship God is to be conscious of His transcendence, hence of His absolute primacy on the human plane; and to have this awareness is to think of Him always, in conformity with the parable

[6] If the human complement of the "Lord" (*Rabb*) is logically the "servant" or "slave" (*ʿabd*), the complement of *Allāh* as such—and He presents Himself *a priori* as the "Infinitely Good" (*Rahmān*) and the "Ever Merciful" (*Rahīm*)—will be man as "vicar on earth" (*khalīfah fī l-ʿard*).

of the unjust judge as well as with the injunction of the Epistle.[7] And this is crucial: "But thou, when thou prayest, enter into thy closet, and when thou has shut thy door, pray to thy Father which is in secret"; according to the Hesychasts, this chamber is the heart, whose door, open onto the world, must be closed. This is quite characteristic of the Christian message, which is a message of contemplative inwardness and sacrificial love, precisely; inwardness being like the consequence—esoteric in varying degrees—of the perspective of love.[8]

"Thy kingdom come": if the hallowing of the divine Name is connected with man's prayer, the coming of the divine Kingdom is linked to God's response; and this we may paraphrase as follows: "Let Thy Name be uttered in a holy manner, that Thy Grace may descend upon us." It could also be said that the first of the two phrases refers to transcendence, and the second, to immanence: indeed, for as the "kingdom of God" is "within you", our first concern ought to be to reach it where it is most immediately accessible to us; for, not only is it impossible for us to realize it *hic et nunc* in the outward world, but every valid and holy work must begin within ourselves, independently of the outward result. And it is not by chance that the phrase concerning the Kingdom comes after that of the hallowing of the Name; the unitive dimension in fact presupposes the devotional dimension; the mystery of transcendence must precede and introduce that of immanence.

This comparison between the relationships of transcendence and immanence leads us to specify a metaphysically crucial point. God is one, and as a result the Transcendent comprises a dimension of immanence, just as for its part the Immanent comprises a dimension of transcendence. On the one hand, the divine Presence in the depths of the sanctified heart, or in the pure intellect, does not lose its transcen-

[7] "And shall God not avenge his own elect, which cry day and night unto him, though he bear long with them? I tell you he will avenge them speedily" (Luke 18:7). "Pray without ceasing (*sine intermissione*)" (1 Thess. 5:17).

[8] The injunction not to "utter vain words" further reinforces this analogy; the "vain" or "many words" indicate outwardness, which can be interpreted at different levels.

dence by the fact of its immanence, since the ego is not identified *tale quale* with the Self; and on the other hand, the transcendence of the creative Principle does not preclude the objective and "existentiating" immanence of the same Principle in creation. In other words: to speak of transcendence is to speak first of all of macrocosm, and to speak of immanence, is to speak *a priori* of microcosm; however, each pole always includes the other, as is shown graphically by the Far Eastern symbol of the *Yin-Yang*, whose testimony we never tire of calling upon in our doctrinal expositions.

On the one hand, there is no transcendence without immanence, for the very perception of transcendence implies immanence in the sense that the knowing subject has to be situated in some fashion at the level of the object known; one can know divine truth only "by the Holy Spirit" which is immanent in the Intellect,[9] otherwise man would not be "made in the image of God". On the other hand, there is no immanence without transcendence: that is to say, the ontological, and in principle mystical, continuity between the immanent Divinity and the individual consciousness in no wise excludes the discontinuity between these two poles which in truth are incommensurable; we could also express this by specifying that union goes from God to man, but not from man to God. Geometrically speaking, what relates to man is the perspective of the concentric circles, which symbolize the modes in the hierarchical arrangement of conformation to the Center; by contrast, what relates to God is the image of the radii, which project the Center in the direction of our emptiness, reintegrating us by that very fact into its Plenitude.

—— ⁘ ——

But let us return, after this digression, to the idea of the divine "Father". This term, as we have said, has a meaning which differs according to whether it relates to man as such or to Christ alone; but it also has a meaning which differs according to whether it is conceived "vertically" or "horizontally": that is to say, according to whether it relates, either to "Beyond-Being" or to Being. In the first case, the "Father" is the pure Absolute and nothing can be associated with Him;

[9] As Meister Eckhart noted, who was not afraid of words, to say the least.

the two other "Persons" already pertain to Relativity, of which they represent the summit; far from pertaining to the manifested world, they, together with the Absolute pure and simple, constitute what we may call the "divine Order". In the second case—which alone has been retained by dogmatic theology—the "Father" is situated at the same level of ontological reality as the other two hypostases; whence the Trinity "Power", "Wisdom", "Love", if one may express it thus.[10] While it is true that this ontological and "horizontal" Trinity does not coincide with the "pure Absolute", it is nonetheless absolute from the point of view of creatures; thus man, when he prays, should not concern himself with the "degrees of reality" comprised in the principial Order, on pain of speaking into the void.

It may be objected that religion has no reason for including the idea of "Beyond-Being", since its aim is the salvation of souls and not metaphysical knowledge, and indeed, as far as its salvific function is concerned, religion can do without the idea in question; but in another respect, that of its claim to absoluteness, it must include it, on pain of misleading—or excluding—certain souls or certain intelligences. One is therefore right in thinking that the word "Father" expresses all that it is capable of expressing, at all levels of doctrine and degrees of understanding. What explains certain dilemmas of dogmatic theology and its recourse to the notion of "mystery"—which amounts to avoiding the question—is precisely the accumulation of unequal perspectives, this accumulation being inevitable since religion must contain everything without for all that having to renounce its specific function.

[10] In Vedantic terms: the "vertical" Trinity corresponds to *Brahma*, *Īshvara*, *Buddhi*; and the "horizontal" Trinity—which is to be found in each of these terms—corresponds to *Sat*, *Chit*, *Ānanda*.

3. David, Shankara, Honen

David, Shankaracharya, and Honen are spiritual personalities who are in many respects quite different, but who have in common the fact that they each represent an altogether fundamental mode of spirituality, and that they do so in a perfect, unsurpassable, and striking manner.

David is the great personification of prayer, of discourse addressed from the depths of the heart to the divine Person. He thus incarnates all the genius of Israel, all the great Semitic message, which is the message of faith; hence all the mystery of man standing before his God, of man having nothing to offer but his soul, but offering it entirely, without reticence or reservation. *De profundis clamavi ad Te Domine*; the creature who stands thus before his Creator knows well what it is to be a human being, and what it is to live here below. David represents the man of virtue contending with the powers of evil, yet invincible because he is a man of God.

It is thus that David, in his Psalms, lays out before us all the treasures of the dialogue between the creature and the Creator. Everything is expressed therein: distress, trust, resignation, certitude, gratitude; and all is combined and becomes a song of glory to the Sovereign Good. It is easy to understand why Jesus is "son of David"; and why—by way of consequence—Mary could be called "daughter" of the Prophet-King,[1] independently of the fact that she is his descendant according to the flesh.

To be a Prophet is to open a way; David, through his Psalms, opened the way of prayer, even though he was not, of course, the first to know how to pray. Metaphysically speaking, he manifested in concrete and human mode—not in abstract and doctrinal mode—the reciprocity between *Māyā* and *Ātmā*; he incarnated so to speak—and this was the purpose of his advent—all the varied and paradoxical play between Contingency and the Absolute, and in this respect he even opened indirectly a way towards gnosis. But he always remains man and, consequently, does not seek to draw away from the human point of view, as is attested notably by Psalm 139:1-6: "O Lord, thou hast

[1] As is attested by the *Magnificat*, which is altogether in the line of the Psalms.

searched me, and known me. Thou knowest my downsitting and mine uprising, thou understandest my thought afar off. . . ." And further: "For there is not a word in my tongue, but lo, O Lord, thou knowest it altogether. Thou hast beset me behind and before, and laid thine hand upon me. Such knowledge is too wonderful for me; it is high, I cannot attain unto it."

Quite apart from the fact that the Psalms must contain implicitly all wisdom,[2] since they are inspired by the divine Spirit, these texts are not lacking in passages capable of directly transmitting esoteric meanings. It is thus that the first of the Psalms speaks of him whose "delight is in the law of the Lord; and in his law doth he meditate day and night". The law of the Lord is, on the one hand, Revelation and, on the other, the Will of God; as for "meditation", its meaning here is that of contemplation and not a cry of the soul. Moreover, this meditative contemplation comprises two modes or two degrees: the "day" and the "night"; the first concerning the literal and immediate truth, and the second, esoteric truth. "The Lord knoweth the way of the righteous; but the way of the ungodly shall perish", for there is no stability, peace, and life save on the side of the Immutable. And the fourth Psalm speaks to us thus: "But know that the Lord hath set apart him that is godly for himself: the Lord will hear when I call unto him." This invocation, in fact, is the very essence of the soul of the righteous, at whatever degree we envisage the prayer of the heart.

Aside from the esoteric allusions necessarily contained in the Psalms, it could also be said, placing ourselves at another point of view, that it is Solomon who represents esoterism most directly; thus David and Solomon appear as two inseparable poles, or as the two sides of one and the same Revelation.

David is the builder of Jerusalem; he represents, for Israel, the passage from nomadism to sedentarism. As for Solomon, he is the builder

[2] We do not, however, believe that one can extract "from any word any meaning one wishes", for hermeneutics has its laws as does every science; but it is a fact that these rules have often been lost sight of.

of the Temple; from David comes the body, from Solomon the heart.[3] Solomon also had sanctuaries built for foreign divinities; through this universalism he came into conflict, not with the formless Truth, but with the Sinaitic, Mosaic, Israelite form of this Truth. That said, we may consider the three Books of Solomon to be a spiritual ascent, the Song of Songs being, in the opinion even of the Cabalists, the summit or the heart—or the wine, in the initiatic sense of the word.

As regards the problem of doctrinal formulation, one should not lose sight of the fact that for the Semites, prior to their contacts with the Greeks, metaphysics pertained in large measure to the inexpressible; now, not to know how to express something—not to know that one can express it or possibly not to wish to express it—is in no wise not to conceive it. And this is all the more the case in a perspective of transcendence where the emphasis is on the fear of God, whence the prohibition of pronouncing the supreme Name; whence too the reticence to articulate the divine mysteries.

—— ·:· ——

In Shri Shankaracharya, the distinction between *Ātmā* and *Māyā* does not appear as a mystery which is highlighted "in the final analysis"; it is expressed without a veil from the outset, which is to say that it constitutes the message itself. As for the veil, which is exoterism, or legalism, Shankara leaves it to others.

Like the inspired Kings of the Biblical world, Shankara is a Prophet, but not the Founder of a religion; his message presupposed a pre-existing framework. This is not to say that his message is merely partial; if it can have this appearance in relation to the Hindu system viewed in its totality, it is because, geometrically speaking, it is like the point which does not encompass the periphery; but it cannot be said that this is because something is lacking in the point, which is perfect and can suffice unto itself. Be that as it may, Providence foresaw for Shankara a quasi-exoteric complement, namely Ramanuja, the great spokesman of Vaishnavite monotheism: the steadfast adversary of the Shankarian and Shaivite metatheism, yet tolerated by the Shankarian

[3] David, however, chose Mount Zion—as a kind of replacement for Mount Sinai—as the seat of the Ark of the Covenant; Solomon placed it in the Holy of Holies.

school as an elementary stage. Even within *Advaita Vedānta*, the necessity for worship is taken into account; indeed, the disciples of Shankara do not deprive themselves of adoring and invoking divinities, for they know that they are human beings and that it is proper to put everything in its place. One cannot transcend *Māyā* without the grace of a divinity which is included within *Māyā*; a divinity who is *Ātmā* of course, but within *Māyā*, as we ourselves are. The contact between man and God presupposes a common ground.

One could speak of the "Shankarian miracle", for this intellectual phenomenon is almost unique in its character at once direct, rigorous, explicit, and integral; just as the Semites, through their Prophets, have brought the great message of Faith to the world, so the Aryans, through Shankara—and in a certain manner also through the Greeks—have brought it the great message of Intellection. This, quite obviously, is not to say that Shankara was the first in India to speak of this mystery, for one finds it formulated first in the *Upanishads*, and later by the great commentator Badarayana; but Shankara offers a particularly precise and complete crystallization of it, unique in its perfection and fruitfulness.

The entire message of the *Upanishads*, of the *Brahma-Sūtras* of Badarayana, and finally of Shankara, may be condensed into the following words: "*Brahma* alone is real; the world is illusion: *Māyā*; the soul is not other than *Brahma*."

Some scholars have quite improperly concluded that the Shankarian advaitism—"non-dualism"—stems in the final analysis from Nagarjuna, hence from Mahayanic Buddhism, which Shankara condemns implacably. The reason for this false comparison is that there is a certain parallelism between advaitism and the Nagarjunan perspective in the sense that both represent a metatheistic immanentism, although the starting points are totally different. No doubt, the Buddhist *Nirvāna* is nothing other than the Self: *Ātmā*; but whereas for the Hindus the starting point is that reflection of the Self which is the "I", for the Buddhists on the contrary the starting point is entirely negative and moreover purely empirical: it is the *Samsāra* as the world of suffering, and this world is merely a "void", *shūnya*, which it is not worth the trouble of trying to explain. The Buddhists deny the concrete existence of the soul and consequently also that of the Self—they conceive in negative mode that which the Hindus conceive in positive mode—and the Hindus, for their part reject no less categorically this negativism of the Buddhists, which appears to them like the negation of the Real itself.

Here one may nonetheless wonder—and we cannot avoid this doctrinally important insertion—why a mind like Shankara "allowed himself to stoop"—as someone maintained—to cast invective even on the very person of the Buddha; now it is excluded that a Shankara could have stooped in any way; in fact, he exercised in this case a function which we will term a "self-defensive symbolist interpretation"; we meet with such examples in the sacred Scriptures themselves. Shankara's mission was not only to formulate the *Advaita Vedānta*, but also to protect the vital milieu of this doctrine from being invaded by Buddhism; but he could not have had the mission of explaining the intrinsic validity of Buddhism, which did not concern the Hindu world. If Shankara's mission had been to explain traditional universality and thereby the validity of all the forms of revelation and spirituality, it could then be said that he erred in judging Buddhism and the Buddha Shakyamuni; but, again, Shankara's mission was altogether intrinsic—not extrinsic as the study of the diverse traditional forms would have been—consequently he could overlook, and wanted to overlook, the possible worth of foreign traditions; he did not practice the "science of religions" (*Religionswissenschaft*).

On the plane of metaphysics as such—and it is this which alone counts in the final analysis—Shankara was one of the most eminent authorities who ever lived on earth; his scope was of a "prophetic" order, as we have said, which means that he was as infallible as the *Upanishads.* The doctrinal and institutional work of Shankara marked the inauguration of a millennium of intellectual and spiritual flowering:[4] to speak of Hindu wisdom is to speak of Shankara.

—— ·:· ——

[4] For he did not limit himself to writing treatises, he also founded spiritual centers whose influence was immense and which still exist in our time.

Like Shankara, Honen Shonin was not the founder of the perspective that he personified, but he was its most explicit and influential representative, and this is precisely what allows us to say that he was the personification of his message. Doubtless—from the point of view of "avataric" phenomenology—he is not situated at the same level as David and Solomon, or as Shankara; the Buddhist equivalent of these rather would be Nagarjuna, the great spokesman of original *Mahāyāna*. But Nagarjuna—while he eminently represented the invocatory branch of *Mahāyāna* and is considered to be the first patriarch of this school[5]—was hardly explicit concerning the perspective here in question; thus it became necessary later on to expound in detail this particular doctrine, and this was done by the other patriarchs of the so-called "devotional" Buddhism. Honen was the seventh and last of them, his predecessors—after the Indian Vasubandhu—were Chinese, followed by one Japanese.[6]

If David incarnates the meeting with God and Prayer, and Shankara metaphysical Truth, Intellection, and Meditation, Honen for his part will be like the incarnation of Faith and Invocation; his perspective and his method coincide, as regards the essential, with the way of the "Russian Pilgrim" and the Hindu *japa-yoga*, as well as with the *prapatti*—saving trust—of the Vaishnavites. This is to say that it is the way of easiness and of Grace; the word "easiness" is not to be taken here in a pejorative sense, but in the sense that the means of this way is technically easy. Grace is conditionally acquired; but concrete perseverance is difficult *de facto*, for in the final analysis it demands all that we are; man cannot bear the "divine climate" for long, except on condition of gently dying to the world and to himself. In fact, no way, if it is really spiritual, could be "easy" in the common sense of the word.

The fundamental idea of the way of Amitabha (Amida in Japanese) coincides in substance with this saying of Christ: "With men it is

[5] Founded on the worship of Amitabha Buddha, the great manifestation of saving Mercy.

[6] Namely, Tan-Luan, Tao-Cho, Shan-Tao, and Genshin. Eminent Japanese precursors who are not counted as patriarchs were Kuya and Ryonin.

impossible, but not with God: for with God all things are possible" (Mark 10:27). This is the Buddhist perspective of the "power of the other" (*tariki* in Japanese), not of "self-power" (*jiriki*); it means that man adopts an attitude of faith "which moves mountains", combined with a divine and sacramental support which, for its part, is what in reality brings about salvation; there is something analogous in the case of Christian communion, which in fact imparts an incommensurable grace without man having any part in it, except as regards receptivity, which clearly has its requirements.

But the sharp alternative between a "way of merit" and a "way of grace"—for that is what the *distinguo* between the principles *jiriki* and *tariki* means in Japanese Buddhism—this alternative is, we think, more theoretical than practical; in concrete reality, there is really more of an equilibrium between the two procedures, so that the distinction evokes the Far-Eastern symbol of the *Yin-Yang*, composed, as is known, by a white half containing a black dot, and a black half containing a white dot, this being the very image of harmonious complementarity.[7] Shinran, the disciple of Honen, wished to place the accent solely on the "power of the other", which from a certain mystical point of view is defensible, on condition of not reproaching Honen for stopping half-way and of having mistakenly maintained an element of "self-power"; for, since initiative and activity are natural to man, we do not see what advantage there would be in depriving him of them. Faith, it seems to us, is much easier to realize if one allows man the joy of collaborating with it; there is in fact a criterion of concrete reality in our personal activity and a guarantee of efficacy, whereas faith alone—as a condition of salvation—rests on nothing which is ours and which we could control. Honen knew as well as Shinran that the cause of salvation is not in our work but in the grace of Amida; but we must somehow open ourselves in some fashion to this grace, otherwise it would suffice to exist in order to be saved.

The great Semitic message, as we have said in speaking of David, is that of faith; now the fact that devotional Buddhism is founded upon saving faith could cause one to think that in both cases it is a question of the same attitude and the same mystery, and consequently that the

[7] For example, man bears in his soul a feminine element, and woman a masculine element; and it is necessarily thus, not only because every person has two parents, but also because each sex belongs to one and the same human species.

two traditional positions coincide. However, aside from the fact that the element of faith exists necessarily in every religion, there is here a *distinguo* to be made: the Semitic or Abrahamic faith is the fervent acceptance of the omnipotent Invisible and consequently submission to its Law, whereas the Amidist faith is trust in the saving Will of a particular Buddha, a trust linked to a particular and well-defined practice, namely the invocation *Namomitābhaya Buddhaya*; or *Namu Amida Butsu*.[8]

Way of altogether human Prayer; way of metaphysical Discernment; way of saving Trust: the three ways can be combined because man has several chords in his soul, or in other words, because human subjectivity comprises different sectors. It is true that Prayer and Trust pertain to the same sector; but such is not the case with metaphysical Discernment, whose subject is not the sensible soul, but pure intelligence, something which—far from creating an antagonism—permits the simultaneity of parallel approaches. The proof of this is the altogether lyrical piety of a Shankara, his hymns and invocations to the feminine as well as masculine aspects of the transcendent and immanent Divinity: to the Self who *a priori* is infinitely "other", but who in reality is infinitely "ourselves".

[8] "Salutation to the Buddha Amitabha". The second of the two formulas cited is the Japanese adaptation of the Sanskrit formula.

4. Fundamental Keys

Meditation, concentration, prayer: these three words epitomize the spiritual life, while at the same time indicating its principal modes. Meditation, from the standpoint where we place ourselves, is an activity of the intelligence in view of understanding universal truths; concentration, for its part, is an activity of the will in view of assimilating these truths or realities existentially, as it were; and finally, prayer is an activity of the soul with respect to God.

These are universal truths, we say; what we have in mind here are the principles that determine everything that is. The first function of intelligence, from the point of view considered here, is to distinguish between the Absolute and the Relative; its second function will be on the one hand the intellectual perception of Relativity insofar as it seems to enter into the domain of the Absolute,[1] and on the other hand the perception of the Absolute as it is reflected in the Relative.

We should specify once more—since the context requires it—that the "pure Absolute" is "the Essence of Essences" or Beyond-Being; as for the Relative, it includes both Being and its central reflection in the world, and then the world itself; Being—or the personal God, the Creator—is the "relative Absolute", if it may be designated thus for want of a less problematical term.

We may thus distinguish in the total Universe four degrees: Beyond-Being, God-Being, Heaven, and Earth, this last term designating symbolically and comprehensively all that is situated below the celestial Summit. Or again: Beyond-Being and Being taken together—if one may say—constitute the divine Principle; while Heaven and Earth constitute universal Manifestation—Heaven being able to be conceived as including Being and Beyond-Being, as is suggested by the expression "Our Father who art in heaven".

But the total Universe is not made up of degrees only, there are modes as well; the former are disposed in "vertical" order, while the latter are in "horizontal" order, while being situated in the appropriate

[1] Or insofar as it appears mysteriously within that which, seen from the standpoint of contingency or of manifestation, is still the Absolute—a paradox that can be explained despite the clumsiness of language, but not explained in a few words.

manner at each of the four degrees. There is first of all a duality: an "active" and divinely "masculine" pole, and a "passive" and divinely "feminine" pole;[2] then comes a trinity: Power, Consciousness, and Felicity.[3] Lastly, we may distinguish a quaternity: Rigor and Gentleness, Activity and Passivity; in other words, Purity or Sacrifice, Goodness or Life, Strength or Light—or victorious Act—and finally Beauty or Peace; herein is to be found the origin of all the Qualities, divine and cosmic.[4]

After meditation, which pertains to Truth and intelligence, comes concentration, which pertains to the Way and the will; there is no Truth that does not have its prolongation in the Way, and there is no intelligence that does not have its prolongation in the will; the authenticity and totality of the values in question require this.

Concentration in itself—that is, apart from its possible contents—ultimately pertains to the "deiformity" of the planes constituting the human microcosm: man is like a tree whose root is the "heart" and whose crown is the "forehead". Now, our mental space—the substance or energy containing or producing thought—is in itself consciousness of the divine Reality; the mind emptied of all coagulations "thinks God" by its very substance, in "holy silence"; man being "made in the image of God".

The same is true of our bodily substance—or more precisely, our consciousness of this substance—actualized in perfect immobility: the very moment we do nothing but "exist", we are virtually identified with Being, beyond all cosmic coagulations. Concurrently with bodily consciousness, there is vital, energetical consciousness, in short, life and movement, which—as sacred dances attest—can be vehicles for

[2] *Purusha* and *Prakriti*, at the level of Being, *Īshvara*; but these poles are reflected also at the other levels, beginning with the supreme *Paramātmā* in which they necessarily have their root.

[3] *Sat*, *Chit*, *Ānanda*, which enter into all existence, although in Vedantic terminology these terms designate only the "dimensions" of *Ātmā* in itself.

[4] Hindu mythology, like every other mythology, designates these Root-Qualities by the names of numerous divinities, the quaternity being moreover the opening onto indefinite differentiation. With the American Indians, the four universal Qualities are manifested mythically by the cardinal points.

our participation in cosmic rhythms and in universal life, at all the levels that are accessible to us through our nature and through Grace.

This leaves, in the human microcosm, the consciousness of self—namely the "heart"— which can likewise be the support of an existential "remembrance of God" on the basis of intellectual, ritual, and moral conditions that guarantee the legitimacy and efficacy of such an alchemy. Whatever the case, the psychosomatic analogies we have just called to mind convey teachings that concern all men: every human being must, out of love of God, strive to "be what he is", to disengage himself from the artificial superstructures that disfigure him and which are nothing other than the traces of the Fall, in order to become once again a tree whose root is made of liberating certitude and whose crown is made of beatific serenity. Human nature is predisposed towards the unitive knowledge of its divine Model; *amore e'l cuor gentil sono una cosa.*

We must now consider another aspect of the question, which is that of contents which are symbols. Mental activity is capable not only of thought but also of imagination, thus of visualizing a symbolic form; in like manner, the mind is sensitive not only to concepts but also to evocative sounds, to auditory symbols; and in like manner again, the body is capable not only of movements that are necessary or useful, but also of symbolic gestures. All this enters into a psychosomatic alchemy of which the spiritual traditions of the East offer us many examples, and of which the Christian liturgies offer echoes. The visual image addresses *a priori* the mind, thus it pertains to the region of the forehead; sound is in connection with our center, the heart; and symbolic movement, quite evidently, concerns the body. And this relates both to the deiform character of the planes constituting the microcosm and to the alchemy of non-discursive, existential symbols—namely forms, sounds, and gestures.

Such is the alchemy of existential participation in the life of the spirit; the mental space participates in it by means of the image, the heart-root through sound, and the body—which is a projection or extension of the two poles—either through immobility and static gesture or through rhythm and dynamic gesture; and we have in mind here basic postures as well as ritual operations accompanied by an awareness of their profound nature.[5] It goes without saying that all

[5] Of which above all Hinduism and Northern Buddhism, with their science of *mantra*, *yantra*, and *mudrā*, possess the secret.

this has its applications in the diverse forms of sacred art or traditional craftsmanship, and sometimes even in legitimate forms of secular art.

Man possesses a soul, and to have a soul means to pray. Like the soul itself, prayer comprises modes and each mode contains a virtue; to pray, then, is to actualize a virtue and at the same time to sow the seed of it. First of all comes resignation to the Will of God: acceptance of our destiny insofar as we cannot and should not change it; this attitude has to become second nature for us, given that there is always something from which we cannot escape. Correlative to this attitude or virtue there is the compensating attitude of trust: whoso puts his trust in God, while conforming to the divine demands, will find God altogether disposed to come to his aid; but what we expect from Heaven we must ourselves offer to others: whoso desires mercy for himself must himself be merciful.

Another compensatory attitude with respect to resignation is the petition for help: we have fundamentally the right, based on our acceptance of destiny, to ask God for this good or that favor; but it goes without saying that we can ask nothing of Heaven if we lack gratitude. Now, to be thankful is to be conscious of all the good that Heaven has given us; it is to appreciate the value of even small things and to be content with little. Gratitude is the complement of supplication, just as generosity is the complement of trust in God. The great lesson of prayer is that our relationship with the world depends essentially on our relationship with Heaven.

IV.
VARIOUS SUBJECTS

1. On the Art of Translating

There is no science of the spiritual without a science of the human, and there is no science of the human without a science of language; this is why it is proper to treat of such secondary things as the art of speaking, of writing, or of translating, in the general context of an anthropology determined by metaphysics and spirituality. As Euripides said: "There is nothing shameful in what is necessary for mortals"; now language is necessary, and small things serve great ones.

The notion of translation has two rather different meanings, depending upon whether we meet with it in the West or in the traditional East; both meanings are legitimate, but they should not be confused. First of all, to make a translation is to convey a discourse, *tale quale*, from one language into another; and it is almost a truism to add that the translation ought to be literal while avoiding faults of grammar and misinterpretations. The translation ought to be literal to the extent that it can be, and because there is no reason for it not to be, since it is a matter of communicating what the author wished to say and nothing else;[1] such is the meaning of the notion of translation in the West, at least in principle, for it is far from being the case that it is always so in fact. In the East, the meaning of the word changes according to the differences in intention, that is to say according to the purpose of the operation: for example, when certain Buddhist texts were translated from Sanskrit into Chinese, the intention was not to offer a linguistic equivalent, it was to enable the Chinese to understand what those texts intended to offer in substance. From this standpoint, the notion of translation coincides with that of commentary: to translate is then at the same time to explain; and nothing prevents readers from having recourse to the original Sanskrit, if they so desire. But this particular perspective should never be introduced into the art of translating in the ordinary and Western sense of the term; one must not confuse divergent intentions or the sufficient reason for these divergences.

[1] Before a court, what is demanded is "the truth, the whole truth, and nothing but the truth"; similarly the translator must communicate "what the author said", "all that the author said", and "nothing but what the author said".

Concerning the plane of translation properly so called—not interpretive commentary—it goes without saying that a translation must always convey the thought of the author; nothing but his thought, all his thought, whether this be expressed by a complex sentence or by a simple expression. But the transfer cannot always convey poetical values, and never euphonic ones: the latter pertain exclusively to the language to be translated, while the former depend, as the case may be, on the grammatical, terminological, and rhetorical resources of that language. This is not to say that a translation removes all the worth of the original text, for the worth of thought is situated beyond linguistic and aesthetic differences. And since thought has priority over style, let alone over euphony, a text that would lose all its worth in a correct translation would thereby prove its own lack of worth. All this amounts to saying that a translation can err, aside from other improprieties, by an over-accentuation of the style to the detriment of the thought; yet there are translators of genius who have succeeded in recreating in the new language not only the stylistic climate, but even the musical element.[2]

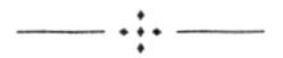

Keeping to the domain of translation in the strict sense, a question arises: how must one translate, in the Bible for example, a word that in the original language comprises an underlying meaning which it does not possess in the language of the translator, so that the meaning of the word is lost in the translation? Many translators are of the opinion that the word has to be replaced by another; we think that on the contrary the word has to be translated literally—except when it is a question of a simple turn of phrase, in which case the word is unimportant—in order to safeguard if need be the symbolism of the image, and adding if necessary a "translator's note" at the bottom of the page, which is altogether normal for a sacred text. For example—in French—we do not accept that the words "rod" and "staff" in Psalm 23 are translated as "support" and "consolation", as has been done,[3] because this commentary destroys

[2] Certain German translations of Dante and Shakespeare have these merits, at least in large measure; this is made easier by the protean side of the Germanic tongue.

[3] In a translation made by the French rabbinate.

the image, which must be kept intact; it can even have its own message to deliver. The same remark applies to the word "to meditate" which, in the translation of the First Psalm,[4] replaces the word "to whisper" of the original; the intention is correct, but the second word designates nonetheless a concrete fact and has its own key symbolism.

A quasi-classic example of a literal translation that is not justified is the Arabic formula rendered in French "may *Allāh* pray on him and grant him a greeting" (*salla 'Llāhu ʿalayhi wa-sallam*), which properly speaking is an absurd translation for two reasons: first of all, "to pray on someone" is meaningless in French; secondly, when one is not sure as to the greeting of a prophet, one bewares of following him. The correct translation of the formula is: "May God bless him and grant him peace"; this last word means here, in contrast to the enlightening and vivifying "blessing", the complementary grace, which is stabilizing and appeasing. The optative indicates, not a void to be filled, but the very nature of the Prophet. The Islamic perspective holds in emphasizing—by means of the optative, precisely—that everything depends on the will of God alone, and that nothing has value without it. Were the *Ave* an Islamic formula, it is quite likely that the casting of *Dominus tecum* would become optative: "May the Lord be with you"; whereas, in reality, what matters is to account for a state of fact and not a wish.

An example of a false and even frankly irritating translation—found in a modern French version of the Koran—is the expression "yo the believers" for "o ye who believe"; this last version—which has been used until now—is the appropriate translation of the Arabic *yā ayyuha 'lladhīna āmanū* (literally: "o ye who are believing"). First of all, the interjection "yo" indicates surprise—good or bad—and not mere hailing; moreover, it absolutely does not convey the dignified and solemn tone of the original Arabic, but on the contrary replaces it with a democratic and casual exclamation that is totally foreign to the Koran in particular and to classical Arabic in general. This obsession with what is "authentic"—always sought downwards and in the direction of the trivial—makes some modern translations as inauthentic as can be.[5]

[4] Rabbinate translation, and also that found in several Christian bibles.

[5] Some will tell us, no doubt, that an "authentic" man is the one who has no "complexes", whereas in fact a normal man cannot help but have some complexes; the man who has none at all is a monster.

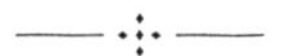

From a somewhat different point of view, it is important not to confuse words that are nobly popular with words that are common and plebeian. Simple, concrete, and everyday words—that can be found in the Bible—should not be replaced by more abstract and learned words; but of course one should use the word that most directly conveys the word to be translated. Similarly, one should never be afraid of using words that are prematurely or arbitrarily considered as being "outmoded", in order to avoid becoming an accomplice of the democratic and demagogic destruction of language; instead of abolishing words that, with a minimum of good will, are perfectly understandable, it is necessary to re-educate readers afflicted with terminological iconoclasm by habituating them to remain faithful to normal language and to take words for what they mean to say. The tendency to attribute "particularizing" and all too often "trivializing" nuances to words, ends up rendering language unusable.

All this brings up the question of "purism": *Le Petit Larousse* defines this word as being "an excessive love for the purity of language characterized by the desire to artificially fix a language at one stage of its evolution, without taking into account the facts of linguistics". First of all, there is no such thing, strictly speaking, as "the facts of linguistics" outside of the facts determining spiritual anthropology, for it is these facts that define and set the limits of the duties and rights of language; therefore one must come to an understanding on the meaning of the notion of "evolution". There are indeed periods during which a language changes under the influence of new ethnic or religious factors: the Latin of Caesar and Cicero no longer corresponded to the mentality of Italy that had become Christianized and partly Germanized; it had therefore the right to evolve. In our day, on the contrary, not merely degeneration pure and simple, but also the deliberate, eager, and crude destruction of language is adorned with the title of "evolution". Be that as it may, in the normal course of things, after natural and legitimate periods of evolution come long periods of stabilization and stability; the safeguarding of the patrimony acquired is the function primarily of the aristocracy, and obviously also—and even above all—of the priesthood which, being the guardian of religion, is thereby also guardian of the dignity of man and of language.

—·:·—

We have noted above that under normal conditions, one must not translate freely, nor interpret or comment, and not paraphrase, except when paraphrasing is required for grammatical reasons. Another crucial rule is the following, taking as an example the French and English languages: when a French turn of phrase, translated into English, is perfectly understandable and contains no error, even though not being the most usual English turn of phrase, there is no reason for replacing it with a "more English" expression, for the French author is not supposed to be an Englishman, and the English reader has the right to notice this, provided it not be at the cost of plain error. This is all the more plausible when the English expression is not only more usual, but also expresses a manner of feeling that is too specifically British; in such a case, it is necessary to avoid this turn of phrase so that a non-English author is not presented psychologically as an average Englishman. Once again, we cite this or that language or this or that people by way of example, for what we say applies to translations generally, whatever the languages being compared; *mutatis mutandis.*

For the rest, it is appropriate to count on the good will of the reader, and thus on a certain tolerance on his part; nothing is more irritating than the falsifications due to a concern for "adaptation", or for "editing" as it is called in English; too often it amounts to treating the reader as being either feeble-minded or a fanatic of the national mentality. The qualitative level of a thought should be maintained: a book addressed to readers that are intelligent does not have to be "adapted" for foreign readers who are not.

We have said that a translation ought to be literal to the extent possible; for the least change risks falsifying or eliminating a shade of meaning. For example, when a French expression or turn of phrase can be conveyed directly as such into English, it should never be conveyed by another one that also exists in French; for if the French author had wished to utilize another turn of phrase he would have done so.[6]

[6] It goes without saying that in speaking of "French" authors we mean all French-speaking authors regardless of their ethnic homeland. Every language comprises ways of thinking and feeling; every man who possesses it assimilates them, at least on the plane of expression if not in depth. Let us note at this point that one meets in every

Doubtless there are linguistic differences that the translator cannot take into account: for example, words of Latin origin express notions; they intend to be definitions and nothing more, at least *a priori*, whereas Germanic words evoke images and experiences. Latin words are ideograms, as it were, whereas Germanic words are more onomatopoeic; the ancient Romans were logicians, and the ancient Germans symbolists, roughly speaking.

Another point to take into consideration is the following: the long sentence, depending on the case, is as legitimate as the short one; thus one should not unhesitatingly replace a cluster of clauses by short formulations the outlines of which might be arbitrary, for then one risks violating logical developments; besides, the psychology of the man who favors long sentences is necessarily different, in some respects, from that of the man who has a predilection for more or less lapidary sentences. For the former, the sentence is a message comprising several branches and various degrees of importance; for the latter, the sentence conveys a fact or an idea, or a single aspect of something complex; in other words, he isolates the constitutive elements of the thought and does not subdivide it in one and the same discourse. It follows that the message of the short sentence ought to be at once whole and homogeneous: the sentence must not contain half of a thought and it must not, moreover, contain two thoughts at once, except when this duality is a bipolarity, in which case unity prevails over duality. Finally, there must be a balance between the sentences: one cannot, in one complex sentence, define the course of a famous man's life, and then, in a short sentence, give the date and place of his death; this information must be inserted into the complex sentence, or else, for consistency's sake, the complex sentence should be subdivided into several independent sentences.

people—and by this we mean a real people and not some political entity—well-known differences in mentality, but which remain within the framework of the ethnic collectivity in question; the German of the South, for example, can be more "Latin" than the German of the North, and the latter more "Scandinavian" than the former, but both have in common the soul that the German language manifests, precisely—the phenomenon of dialects changes nothing in all this.

From the standpoint of the art of translation, it goes without saying that in translating, one cannot transform a text made up of long sentences into another made up of short sentences, although in certain cases one sometimes has to find a middle way. Whatever the worth of the short sentence as such may be—or in a monosyllabic language such as Chinese—it is undeniable that the barbarism of our time prefers the shortened sentence, whereas ancient intellectuality—or even still nineteenth century thought—readily expresses itself by the long and complex sentence, with the exception of lapidary sayings, the very content of which requires brevity. These observations are necessarily approximate, for not every barbarian prefers the short sentence nor is every man who does a barbarian; and other reservations of the kind.

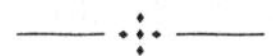

Every language is a soul, said Aristotle; that is to say, a language is a psychic or mental dimension. There are languages that are parallel, such as French and Italian, as there are those that are complementary, such as French and German; in other words, there are linguistic families, hence types, that on the one hand include and on the other exclude. Quite obviously, the possession of complementary languages is more enriching than that of parallel languages: Meister Eckhart, in his writings and thus in his soul, felicitously combined the symbolic and imaginative power of the Germanic with the clear rationality and precision of the Latin. This amounts to saying that every man—since mankind is one—bears within himself the virtuality of all languages and thus all souls.

But there are not only neutral differences, there are also qualitative differences: the ancient languages are qualitatively equivalent, not in the sense that they do not each possess their distinctive qualities, but in the sense that all possess a general quality allowing them to serve as a liturgical language, which precisely is not the case with modern languages; and it is a great pity that all too many theologians are unaware of this, in the Greek Church as well as in the Latin Church. In a certain sense, all the ancient languages are sacred, for the simple reason that language is so, at least *a priori*; the profanity of language is a specifically modern phenomenon, whose causes coincide with those of modernity as such. This is to say that modern languages lack universality and primordiality because they are marked by individualism and all the hypertrophies and atrophies resulting from it; which does not mean that they are unable to express the highest truths, at least with respect to logic if not with respect to the atmosphere of the sacred. Unquestionably, the languages marked by humanism excel in expressing psychological subtleties, but that is a kind of abuse, since too often these subtleties have no right to exist and in any case ought not to be taken into consideration.

It may be objected that there are also so-called "primitive" languages not fixed in writing; they are no doubt very unequal, but what matters here is that they have never undergone the influence of anti-metaphysical and "profaning" ideologies; even the most deprived of peoples have kept the sense of the sacred.

As for the European languages, there are all told three degrees to consider: firstly the degree of Greek, Latin, Gothic, Slavonic, which is almost that of sacred languages;[7] secondly the degree of the Italian of Dante or the German of Meister Eckhart, which is at the edge of liturgically utilizable languages; and thirdly the degree of the European languages after the seventeenth or eighteenth century more or less, which no longer fulfill the requisite conditions for liturgical usage.

All these *distinguos* do not prevent human language as such from being, by definition, something sacred; thus it is a true betrayal to neglect this or even to push it into the abyss, as is so cheerfully done in our times. One of man's first duties is to speak and write correctly, hence also in a noble fashion, always keeping one's gaze fixed on tradition, which represents and channels the divine origin; even profane languages, which are our own, have in themselves safeguarded that essential element—basically natural to man—which is dignity. The same is not true for demagogic jargons forced upon us in the name of a cult of sincerity inspired by the real or supposed vulgarity of the masses, and in any case propagated by the mass media;[8] on the one hand, it is decided that the people are trivial—forgetting that all men

[7] It may be that the boundary line is sometimes uncertain.

[8] This evil affects English and German much more than the Latin languages. In German, "trivialization" goes hand in hand with the abolition of the Gothic script, the only one fit for the imaginative character of this language, but "anachronistic" from the standpoint of the internationalist barbarism of our time. In French, the perfectly unnecessary introduction of English expressions denotes the same tendencies.

are not alike—and on the other hand triviality is forced upon them, it being considered as the human norm, whereas in fact it results from irreligion, hence from the loss of the sense of the sacred.

As we have noted above, it is appropriate to distinguish carefully, in the domain of language as well as in others, between evolution and degeneration; in the Mediterranean countries, for example, the Christian religion on the one hand and the influence of the Germanic element on the other, have determined, starting from a basis of Latin which is *a priori* Italic and pagan,[9] a certain necessary and providential evolution, so much so that the language of Dante presents itself legitimately as a new language.[10] And this has no connection with the popular carelessness and laxity characteristic of most dialects, nor with all the more reason with the systematic destruction of languages.

Thus our interest for the least linguistic matters is explained by the connection between language and spiritual factors. Language is man, and it is therefore our deiformity; to speak is to be "made in the image of God", and *noblesse oblige.* Man's first word was a prayer, and could not but be one; the creature is a mirror of the Creator. We could also say that the first word uttered by man was the Name of the Eternal, in answer to the creative Word that projected a divine image into the world.

[9] This epithet means that the flattening of Roman religion necessarily influenced the quality of the language.

[10] What Dante termed *il dolce stil nuovo*, "the sweet new style". Sweet because more melodious, more full of imagery, and also closer to religious and contemplative sensibility than that language of logicians, jurists, administrators, military men, and chroniclers that is Latin; without forgetting that every correct language becomes spiritualized through its content.

2. Message of a Vestimentary Art

Dress, like language and vertical posture, is one of the prerogatives of man; although doubtless much less important than the two other prerogatives mentioned, it is not less characteristic of *homo faber.* Man is made of intelligence, will, and sensibility; he needs a congenial physical ambience, starting with a framework for the person he is: dwelling, tools, and then art objects properly so called. No doubt, the notion of dress is both relative and complex; the quasi-nudity of certain human groups—whether "civilized" or nor—pertains to that same notion to the extent that the vestimentary minima as well ornaments respond to the need of framing the bodily form, the "attire" having as a function either to veil the body or on the contrary to accentuate its symbolism or beauty.

The existence of princely and priestly garments proves that clothing confers a personality upon man, that is to say it expresses or manifests a function which may transcend or ennoble the individual. The type of clothing, in manifesting a function, represents thereby its corresponding qualities; although costume does not of course change man *ex opere operato*, yet for the person normally predisposed for this—therefore sensitive to duties and moral qualities—clothing actualizes a given awareness of the norm and a given conformity to the archetype, thus to primordiality and universality.[1] It goes without saying that man should only put on the kind of attire to which he is entitled in one degree or another; usurpation is as demeaning as vanity; and "*noblesse oblige*".

This calls for the following remark: the forms bearing witness to an ethnic genius and to a religious perspective always surpass the average state of those who carry them; the proof of this is the underestimation one finds in almost all peoples—either effectively or virtually—of their traditional arts which they betray with disconcerting

[1] "If a French proverb says that 'a cowl does not a monk make' there exists a German proverb which says exactly the opposite: *Kleider machen Leute*, clothes make the man. . . . Everyone can observe how the quality of a particular type of clothing modifies our behavior: it is because the individual tends to efface himself before the function, so that he is as it were remodeled by the costume" (Jean Hani, *La Divine Liturgie*, chap. "*Dramatis Personae*").

facility. Be that as it may, one could wish this world here below were like a museum wherein peoples would display nothing but their most beautiful things, but this would already be the celestial world; it is nevertheless a kind of realism and also of nobleness to cling above all else to the perception of the archetypal and quasi-divine intentions of things. In certain respects, the dream of the poet and the realism of the wise man meet: the aesthete—if his intelligence protects him from a certain shortsightedness—is always more realistic than the man who is trivial, ungrateful, and blasé.

Clothing in itself may represent that which veils, thus exoterism; however, through its symbolic elements, its sacerdotal language precisely, it becomes interiorized and "esoterized". In that case, clothing in its turn represents the soul or the spirit, hence the inward, in which case the body stands then for our material and terrestrial existence only; this it does implicitly and by comparison—not in itself and viewed outside of a vestimentary context—for the spiritual primacy of a given attire derives from a more contingent and "less ancient" viewpoint than the spiritual primacy of the body.

According to some, the celestial Virgin who brought the sacred Pipe to the Red Indians was clad in white; according to others she was naked; the white color and nudity both refer to purity, primordiality, and essentiality, hence also to universality.

Our intention here is to discuss a vestimentary style almost unknown and insufficiently appreciated, but quite expressive and even fascinating, that of the Indians of the North American Plains; in so doing, we do not have the feeling of confining ourselves to too restricted a subject, since to speak about a given art is always to speak about art as such, not to mention that this subject opens in fact onto considerations that are of a general interest to everyone.

When we stand in the middle of a plain, three things strike our vision: the immense circle of the horizon, the immense vault of the sky, the four cardinal points. It is these elements which primordially determine the spirit and soul of the Indians; one could say that their entire metaphysics or cosmology is based upon these initial motifs. The son of the famous Black Elk explained to us that the entire religion of the Indians can be represented by a circle containing a cross; the Great Spirit always works in circles, his father had said, and the cross is the well-known doctrine of the four directions of space, upon which is founded the rite of the sacred Pipe. Circle of the Earth, circle of the Sky; East, South, West, North.

The art of the Plains Indians makes extensive use of these symbols. We are thinking here *a priori* of two particularly important motifs: the great sun, whose rays are eagle feathers, and which may be composed of several concentric circles, and the rosette embroidered with porcupine quills which often adorns the garments.[2] These quills in themselves symbolize the rays of the sun, which adds one more magical quality to the solar pattern. The designs of these rosettes consist of a combination of circles and radii, and are thus always an image of the sun or the cosmos; in this last case, the cruciform diagram represents both the four directions of space and the four phases of time: of the day, the year, life, and the cosmic cycle. And let us recall that the concentric circles and the centrifugal radii, in the embroidered rosettes as well as in the feathered suns, represent respectively the ontological or cosmic relationships of discontinuity and continuity, transcendence and immanence.

The eagle feather, like the eagle itself, represents the Great Spirit in general and the divine presence in particular, as the Sioux explained it to us; thus it is plausible that the rays of the sun, itself the image of the Great Spirit, would be symbolized by feathers. But these very stylized feathers forming the sun of concentric circles also represent the cocoon, symbol of vital potentiality; now life and solar radiation coincide for obvious reasons.

One of the most powerful symbols of the sun is the majestic headdress made of eagle feathers; he who wears it is identified with the solar orb, and it is easy to understand that not everyone is qualified to wear it; its splendor—unique in its kind among all traditional headdresses in the world—suggests both royal and priestly dignity, thus the radiance of the hero and the sage.[3]

[2] In the nineteenth century, glass beads imported from Europe were more and more used for the embroideries, and this gave rise to a new style but not at the expense of authenticity.

[3] According to the French authors Thévenin and Coze it is "the most majestic headdress ever conceived by the human genius" (*Moeurs et Histoire des Indiens peaux-rouges*). Sometimes the feather bonnet is adorned with the horns of the buffalo, which adds

The garb of the chief or the hero suggests the eagle soaring towards the sun: the nature of the eagle is to fly upwards, hence also to see things from afar, from "above" precisely: the eagle soars and then circles in a luminous solitude. The Sun Dance realizes the ascension of the royal bird towards the solar luminary; this evokes the Hindu *deva-yāna* and the Islamic *sirāt al-mustaqīm*. When the Indian prays, he extends his arms upwards, like a bird taking wing.

According to an almost universal tradition, the eagle itself symbolizes the sun; this precisely is expressed by the eagle-feather bonnet. Formerly, each feather had to be earned: the identification of man with the solar orb demands a heroic drama. This is demonstrated by the Sun Dance which implies a multiple victory over the lower *māyā*, that of the world and that of the ego, spiritually speaking.

In this context one may think of the Hindu Garuda, the eagle messenger of the gods, the mount of Vishnu; Garuda is the first of the worshippers of this Archangel-God,[4] he is like the eagle soaring towards the sun. He is also called *Amritā-harana*, "he who has appropriated the Nectar (*Amrita*) for himself", *Gaganeshvara*, "Lord of Heaven", and *Nāgāntaka*, "Destroyer of the serpents", the victor over terrestrial *māyā* in all its aspects. With the Greeks, Hermes has an analogous meaning, which is indicated by the wings adorning his shoulders, his feet, and his hat; he is the Mercury of the Romans, who gave his name to the planet nearest the sun.

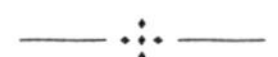

A very typical element of Indian dress are the fringes; they first of all evoke rain, which is already a very important image since rain is a message from heaven to earth. But the fringes also symbolize the spiritual fluid of the human person—his *orenda*, as the Iroquois would say, or his *barakah*, as the Arabs would say. This observation is all the more

to it a pontifical symbol. The feathered spear—the solar ray—prolongs the headdress in a dynamic and combative mode.

[4] The "Triple Manifestation" (*Trimūrti*) is indeed situated at the archangelical degree; the "White Buffalo Woman", who is the equivalent of Lakshmi, belongs to the same celestial realm. We heard, on the part of Christian Indians, that the White Buffalo Woman is identified with the Virgin Mary, a remark which in itself is not lacking in profundity.

plausible when one thinks that, instead of the fringes, Indian shirts are often decorated with horsehair or with scalps;[5] now hair, as is well known, is the vehicle of a magical power, an *orenda* precisely. We could also say that the fringes are derived from the feathers of a bird, of the eagle above all: arms adorned with fringes are "magically" and spiritually equivalent to the wings of an eagle. Sometimes ermine skins are added to the fringes, thus conferring upon them a quasi-royal symbolism, the ermine being everywhere considered as a sign of majesty.

The most diverse objects may be adorned with embroideries and fringes; one of the most important is the bag containing the "Peace Pipe" and the ritual tobacco, the latter's function being to sacrifice itself by burning and to rise towards the Great Spirit. This bag was brought to the Indians, together with the Pipe, by the "White Buffalo Woman" (*Pté-San-Win* in Lakota); it is she—or rather her celestial prototype, *Wohpé*—who makes the smoke and our prayers rise towards Heaven.

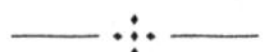

Pictorial art in the widest sense—we mean by this the animation of surfaces by means of colors, be it by paintings properly so called, or by drawings, engravings, and embroideries—comprises essentially two dimensions or modes, the figurative and the decorative, both occurring occasionally in the vestimentary art of the Indians as well as in the decoration of their tents. The first mode is executed by the men, the second by the women, which is full of meaning: in effect, the figurative art refers to what is determined—or central in a certain sense—and the decorative art to what is undetermined and extensive or to all-possibility; and this apart from the particular meanings that either the figurative drawings or the geometrical motifs may have. Or again: the figurative art expresses the content of our consciousness, the decorative art our substance; thus it is that man represents an idea whereas woman embodies a manner of being, an existential *materia* in which the idea may fix itself and blossom; this is the complementarity between Truth and Virtue.

[5] As is proven by history, the sense of the sacred does not exclude ferocity, with the Red Indians any less than with the Zenist samurai or with our very Christian knights of the Middle Ages.

Art is in a general way both a means of expression and a means of assimilation: expression of our qualitative—not arbitrary and chaotic—personality, and assimilation of the archetypes thus projected; it is therefore a movement from ourselves to ourselves, or from the immanent Self to transcendent Being, and conversely; a purely empirical "ourselves" means nothing, all values being rooted in the Absolute.

Doubtless, our Indians have no sacred art properly so called apart from that ritual object of primary importance which is the sacred Pipe;[6] nonetheless, they possess to the highest degree the sense of the sacred, and they replace the element "religious art" with what we could call a "liturgy" of virgin Nature.

Plains Indian attire "humanizes" virgin Nature, it transmits something of the immensity of the prairies, the depth of the forests, the violence of the wind, and other affinities of the kind.[7] That said, it would be wrong to object—as professional "demystifiers" like to do—that Indian dress had only a limited social and practical bearing, that not all individuals wore it, all the more so since for the Red Indians nudity too had a value both practical and symbolical; what matters here is not the fluctuation of the modalities, but rather the ethnic genius which, if it finds different modes of exteriorization, remains always true to itself and to its fundamental message.

It is a curious fact that many people love the Indians but do not dare admit it, or admit it with conventional reservations while ostentatiously disidentifying themselves from Rousseau's "good savage" as well as from Cooper's "noble savage", and above all from any kind of "romanticism" or "aestheticism"; without forgetting the concern of not being taken for a child. As for the "noble savage", he is not

[6] Neither did Shintoism have a figurative art before the arrival of Buddhism.

[7] The vestimentary art of the Forests was analogous—not quite similar—to that of the Plains, but it was rapidly modified upon contact with the whites; without a doubt, the floral motifs which characterize the embroidery of the Forest Indians and even of some tribes of the Northern Plains is due to the white influence. It should not be forgotten that many of the Plains Indians had come from the Forests and established themselves in the prairies relatively lately.

altogether "drawn out of thin air", if only for the simple reason that all martial peoples who habitually and by vocation confront suffering and death and who have a cult of self-domination and dignity, possess nobleness and grandeur by the very nature of things. Such peoples—or such castes—distinguish themselves also by their hospitable customs, but none surpass, or perhaps even equal, the Red Indians in this respect; one of the fundamental qualities of the Indians in fact is their liberality combined with their scorn of riches, a quality which compensates for their warlike aggressiveness. The Indian of heroic times was not only hospitable, he also loved to give and sometimes gave almost everything he possessed; the "give-aways", where gifts are exchanged with greatest generosity, are still being practiced nowadays.

The prestige enjoyed by the Indians in the most diverse milieus and countries is explained by the truly fascinating coincidence of moral and aesthetic qualities, by the combination of a both stoic and intrepid courage and the extraordinary expressiveness of their physiognomies, clothing, and implements. The fact that the Indian is perpetuated in children's games all over the world and sometimes in adult games, cannot be an accident devoid of meaning; it indicates a cultural message of powerful originality, a message which cannot die and which survives, or rather radiates, as best it can.

As far as the properly spiritual message is concerned—which shares a remote kinship with the shamanism of the Far East, including Shinto—it survives in that universal prayer that is the rite of the sacred Pipe and in the Sun Dance, the sacrificial rite for the renewal of man and the world. One should also mention a rite of purification, the "sweat lodge", which resembles the Finnish sauna, and then too, and above all, the solitary invocation atop a hill; or the possibly wordless prayer of the naked Indian who, with his arms raised towards the sky, bathes in the infinitude of the Great Spirit.

After all these considerations on various aspects of the Red Indian culture, it does not seem inappropriate to present a few reflections on the tragic destiny of this ethnic group. All told, what caused the ruin of the red race and its tradition in the nineteenth and the beginning of the twentieth century, was the abrupt alternative between the two notions of the "civilized" and the "savage", each term being taken as an absolute; this made it possible to attribute every value to the white man and leave nothing to the red man, so much so that, according to this perspective, the latter no longer had any right to exist, and this was exactly the conclusion people wanted. The "noble red man" has been much derided, and still is so; but this notion is the only one that counteracts the stupid and criminal alternative pointed out above, and this proves in a certain way the correctness of the notion in question. Indeed, nobleness is a value which stands completely above this alternative and which reminds us that a man is man before being either "civilized" or "savage", and that, consequently, any normal and normative human category possesses the dignity of man, with all the possibilities of worth and greatness this dignity implies.

When the difference between the "civilized" and the "savage" is reduced to normal proportions, one arrives at the complementarity—and equilibrium—between the "city dweller" and the "nomad" about which Ibn Khaldun has spoken with much insight, recognizing in each of the two societies a positive function in the economy of human possibilities. And this also applies to a case like America where, quite obviously, each ethnic group would have had something to learn from the other, something precisely that the whites were absolutely not disposed to admit. On the side of the Indians, the difficulty did not come from an automatic prejudice, it came on the one hand from the fact that they were being mistreated by "civilization", and on the other, from the fact that the values of this civilization were—and are—to a great extent compromised by the modern deviation; the whites, all too preoccupied with "things", have forgotten what man is, while being "humanists"; but it is for that very reason that they have forgotten it.

—— ·:· ——

It could also be said that the red man—in reality a Mongol emigrated from Siberia more than ten thousand years ago—has been a victim of the democratic system and its blind mechanism. In practice, democracy is the tyranny of the majority; the white majority, in America, had no interest in the existence of this red minority, and therefore the army, which in certain cases should have defended the rights of the Indians—rights solemnly guaranteed by treaties—defended the interests of the whites contrary to these agreements. Democracy entails demagogy; in such a climate a popular criminality "in fact" becomes a governmental criminality "by right", at least when the victim is situated outside the collectivity included in a given democratic legality. Doubtless, the Red Indians were not "citizens", but they were "compatriots", to say the least; their status should have in any case been specified juridically on the basis of this definition. A monarch—or, quite paradoxically, a military dictator—could have ensured interracial justice, a democratic president could not; even a man as profoundly noble and morally courageous as Lincoln would have been paralyzed, in this respect, had he been given time to take care of the Indians as he had intended.

All things considered, if it is absurd to call an unmistakable and organized genocide a "fatality of history", it is equally absurd to accuse the "Americans"—and them alone—of having killed the red man, for there are no "Americans"; the inhabitants of the New World are European immigrants, no more no less, and it is not these immigrants who invented "civilizationism" and democracy. The Indian, inasmuch as he embodies virgin Nature, the sense of the sacred, and the scorn of money, had been murdered in Europe, in the minds of men, independently of the conquest of the new continent; and if the Indian had his defenders and friends in Europe, he has had them well before in America itself.

3. Concerning a Question of Astronomy

One cannot legitimately compare Ptolemy's astronomy with that of Copernicus without *a priori* taking into account their respective foundations and intentions. The geocentric system, including the cosmological and spiritual speculations connected with it, is based on natural—and profoundly providential—appearances, and on symbolism; the heliocentric system, for its part, is based on physical facts and on the desire to know. The first system cannot be separated from integral anthropology; the second intends to remain independent of all human subjectivity and concern itself solely with objective reality.

Unquestionably, the geocentric system is right from the standpoint of its own basis: the appearance of the sun rising in the East and setting in the West, or that of the stellar vault outlining the same movement, is so habitual to man that it is part of his nature; it cannot be due to chance any more than man is, and that is why it can serve as the basis for a science which is "exact" within its order, and one just as complex as the human microcosm.[1] But this does not mean, quite obviously, that the heliocentric system is false; besides, the desire to know and therefore to explore is no less natural to man; it is found in all traditional climates, although often with questionable results. This desire to explore is legitimate so long as it is not accompanied by abusive speculations and does not become involved in paths which exceed *de facto* average human capacities, both psychologically as well as intellectually; conversely, the standpoint of a man who relies on "ancestral" and "traditional" natural appearances is legitimate as long as it does not set itself absurdly against empirical evidence.

By the nature of things, the sacred Scriptures—and with them the traditional mentality— have always shared a solidarity with geocentrism, but this does not mean that they are intrinsically contrary to the facts discovered by profane science and that, consequently, these facts

[1] For the most ancient Greeks as for the Vedic Hindus, the earth was a disk; later, with Pythagoras, Aristotle, and Anaximander, the prevailing image was that of a spherical earth, but always central and immobile. The heliocentrism of Aristarchus had no success and it was the cosmography of Ptolemy which dominated men's minds up to Copernicus.

must be rejected in the name of tradition and the sacred; for it is a question here of conditional, not absolute, solidarity. If the Scriptures are geocentrist, that is because God is only interested in that which is for man's real and ultimate good;[2] God has no interest in cosmic facts that man cannot observe under "normal" conditions and that—if he is able to discover them thanks to "abnormal" circumstances—he is incapable of reconciling with spiritual symbolisms and of assimilating without plunging into the inhuman; we are speaking here of the average man, for man as such can know all that is knowable, and consequently all that is. The inhuman coincides with the false because man's reason for being is perception, not of every possible phenomenon of course, but of the essential real.

Scientific curiosity has always existed, we repeat; but, under normal conditions, it has always ceded pride of place to more important and more realistic interests, namely, metaphysical science and religion, pure intellection and saving faith. It has been said that the data of modern astronomy favors atheism; which is true *de facto*, not through any fault of this data—no one is obliged to become an atheist because he understands that the earth turns around the sun—but through the fault of men who are incapable of situating this data correctly; or of integrating it into a metaphysical perspective that combines the message of geocentric symbolism with the facts—likewise symbolical in their fashion—observed by an astronomy armed with telescopes. It should be noted, moreover, that the great astronomers of the Renaissance were sincere believers; and so, too, prior to them, were the Muslim astronomers.

An argument in favor of geocentrism could be the fact that the earth is the dwelling place of man—of the pinnacle-creature whose spirit is "central" and therefore total—and that consequently our planet takes precedence over other celestial bodies. It would thus be logical for those bodies to revolve around the earth; the real astronomical situation would merely be the mechanism—*a priori* hidden—of a superior reality which God offers to man. All this is true in its own order,[3] but it does not abolish the reality of the "mechanism" nor the fact that this mecha-

[2] Whence the "noble naivety" (*die edle Einfalt*) of holy Scripture, according to an expression of Schiller.

[3] It should not be forgotten, however, that other planets—possibly situated in other "solar" systems—may be inhabited by beings analogous to man, which weakens considerably the argument in question.

nism in turn inevitably manifests a cosmological and metaphysical situation, since all that exists is a message of truth. Man, in this respect, is merely a neutral witness of a materialized ontology; in that case, the majesty of the object takes precedence over that of the subject.

All that we have just said shows that it is aberrant to wish to make of the Ptolemaic system an astronomy in the sense of the so-called exact physical science—which it is from the standpoint of registering perceptible phenomena—and to wish to oppose thus the geocentrism of the ancients, *de facto* inevitably "traditional", to the heliocentrism of the moderns. The concept of a sun revolving around the earth is absurd because it is inconceivable that a mass-energy so relatively immense as the sun should revolve around a globe so small as the earth; it is absurd ontologically as well as physically. Certainly, the ancients could not know this disproportion; they could not measure either the expanse of the terrestrial "plain", or the size of the sun in relation to this expanse, any more than they could conceive of the physical consequences of the real situation. But they compensated for this ignorance by metaphysical knowledge which, precisely, the moderns totally lack and which obviously takes precedence over knowledge of physical facts.

Eminent scholars, it appears, have observed that, all things considered, it is not possible to say which of the two, Ptolemy or Copernicus, is right; we can well imagine that the effort to penetrate to the limits of space, of matter, of energy—we will not discuss the bearing of these notions—could give rise to a "vertigo" allowing one to think that there is no center anywhere and that no thing can be said to revolve around anything else. But the subtleties of the theory of relativity—plausible or not as the case may be—remain outside the question at issue here, given that our planetary system, or even the entire galaxy, represents a cosmos in which the relation of a center and a periphery exists indisputably.

As traditionalist as one may be, the theory of relativity cannot come to the rescue of Ptolemy, any more than of a drunk, stumbling around a lantern, who believes that it is the lantern which is moving around him; in short, the greatest of physicians could never abolish the notions of center and periphery, nor even more of the universal—and properly "meta-physical"—principles to which these notions refer.

—·:·—

Thus, so-called "exact" profane science has its efficacy and therefore its rights; an entirely different question is that of philosophical and ostentatious scientism. The "classical" vices of the latter are, first of all metaphysical ignorance and then, by way of consequence, empiricism and materialism, the one just as exclusive as the other: it is thus that modern science, due to prejudice, is ignorant of the principle of cosmic cycles on the one hand, and of the degrees of universal manifestation on the other; it is unaware of the fact that the universe is in substance a kind of "divine respiration"—Hinduism is very explicit in this respect—and that matter is nothing but a shell that conceals cosmic substances that are more and more real following an ascending order. But this ignorance, we must insist, does not prevent the discoveries of astronomers from corresponding to realities in their own order, thus to symbols; unquestionably, the central position of the sun manifests the priority of the Supreme Principle.[4]

In other words: a cosmic degree—such as the physical world—is like a circle around a more "interior" and ontologically superior circle that determines it and can even determine it, incidentally, in a completely exceptional, "supernatural", and miraculous manner; this precisely is what escapes modern physicists, whence that ersatz which is transformist evolutionism. In a similar manner, a cosmic cycle is like a rotation around a more "interior" or more primordial rotation, each of the possible rotations being determined by a ray which emanates from the absolute Center and which decides the rhythms of the temporal phases. The system of concentric circles constituting the world—as well as the spiroidal movement of the cycles—is either projected or reabsorbed according to the archetypal intentions of the absolute Center; the intellect makes it possible to conceive of it, but this obviously escapes investigations of a purely physical order.

[4] As Kepler observed. We have read somewhere that the sun is not situated exactly at the center of the planetary trajectories—which could be explained by the influence of the galactic context—but this does not alter the fact that the position of the sun is definitely central.

Returning now to the idea which was our point of departure, we would say the following: the comparison between the doctrine of Ptolemy and that of Aristarchus or of Copernicus teaches us that there are essentially two kinds of appearances, namely the appearance that corresponds to a substance and functions as a symbol, and the appearance that corresponds to an accident and is merely an illusion of no importance; thus, the rising of the sun represents a fundamental teaching, whereas a mirage in the desert amounts to a mere optical error. One could also claim that the apparent movement of the sun and the starry heavens constitutes a divine message, whereas the movement of the earth around the sun is only the mechanism of this message, at least with respect to man. God cannot lie to us, which means—as we said above—that the earthly appearances habitual to man are providential and manifest a fundamental spiritual message; this is precisely what makes it possible to erect sciences based on images of this sort. The language of Scripture and of myths bears witness to the same principle, and that is why it is futile to reproach the revealed texts for having some naive elements; symbolism takes precedence over the fact envisaged as such. It is nevertheless quite obvious that the symbolism in question could not be a closed system: the wall of appearances can be broken, either accidentally or by exploration, and what is discovered in this manner, far from belying the profound message of the appearances and thus their divine intention—even though there is formal antinomy—transmits in its turn a celestial message.

On the one hand, man is the measure of all things, and this is indeed his reason for being; it is what Genesis teaches us. On the other hand, man necessarily represents a specific subjectivity, thus a limitation: truth, while inscribed in our intellective substance, nevertheless exists outside and above us. This means that man can be right in two ways, either by being perfectly himself, or on the contrary by disregarding his subjectivity altogether; the whole question is to know in what way or at what level we envisage either the subject or the object. By definition, what is most profoundly and authentically human rejoins the Divine.

APPENDIX

Selections from Letters and Other Previously Unpublished Writings

1

It is typical of the European bourgeois culture that everything is "overadorned": it is indeed incredible to see how much knowledge and expertise is pumped into men—all for nothing—and how much time and effort and thinking is spent on things which are not at all proportioned to such an effort; seen in purely mental terms, the knowledge of an Aristotle cannot be compared to the contents of the mind of a child who goes to the conservatory, but who before God is not one hundredth of what an Aristotle is! This lack of the sense of proportions, this cult of the excessive, of the overadorned is also, as just mentioned, a distinguishing feature of Western degeneracy. On the other hand, it is clear as day that a person, who needs "*Etudes*" and "*Nocturnes*" for his inner equilibrium, has no sense for nature—I mean for nature as it is in itself, not seen as the background for a psychic life that is artificial, overwrought, and "civilized".

2

If I sharply reject the modern world as such—although I am only partially in agreement with Guénon's *Orient et Occident*—it is because I am fundamentally opposed to philosophical rationalism and also to artistic naturalism; both are hallmarks of "classical" Greece and appeared anew as the "Renaissance". There are two things here that I would like to note: it is false to see in Plato a rationalist in the modern sense of the term; Anaxagoras and Protagoras could not stand farther apart from him; influenced by Egypt, he also criticized naturalistic art. Paradoxically, there was also a renewed interest in Plato and Plotinus in the Renaissance; also good poetry and good music. Be this as it may: that I reject modernism as a general phenomenon does not mean, quite obviously, that I do not recognize isolated instances of individual worth in these latter times. But no one, in full awareness of the facts, could deny that the main characteristic of our time is a desacralization of the whole world.

3

"Cosmology" is a general term which belongs to the metaphysical perspective as well as to the creationist viewpoint and to modern science. So we can distinguish between a cosmology which is metaphysical, another which is theological or creationist, and a third which is materialistic. Given that the theory of evolution is intrinsically false, there can be no question of a reconciliation of these views.

Evolution exists in the sense that a seed becomes a root and then a tree, but not in the sense that an oak tree becomes a pine tree. Evolution is the unfolding of a given virtuality and not the passage of a given possibility to a quite different possibility. Modern science is right when it describes the succession of geological periods but not when it tries to describe the origin of life or of intelligence. Modern cosmology cannot be something other than geology, paleontology, and astronomy; and there exists not the least difficulty in combining them either with Semitic creationism or with Indo-Greek emanationism, for the simple reason that facts are always compatible with principles.

The metaphysical viewpoint is scientific, and so is the geological, paleontological, and astronomical viewpoint. As for the creationist viewpoint, it is not scientific, but symbolist.

4

Your classification is certainly plausible according to a certain perspective; but it is no less plausible that differences in perspective can bring about differences in the allocation of the symbols, if one may say. For example, Guénon paradoxically attributes childhood to the North and to winter, youth to the East and to spring, maturity to the South and to summer, and old age to the West and to autumn; one could just as easily attribute childhood to the East and to spring, youth to the South and to summer, maturity to the West and to autumn, and old age to the North and to winter; for childhood, like spring, is incontestably the time of blossoming forth and of joy; summer is the time of heat, love, passion, which corresponds aptly to youth; maturity, like autumn, is the time of the harvest, plenitude, achievement; and old age, which has always been compared to winter, is the time of detachment, contemplation, purity.

Guénon wrote to you that he doubts "that one can establish a strict correlation with the faculties"; I suppose he has mental faculties in mind. But one can hold a different opinion and attribute reason to the North, sentiment to the South, imagination to the East, and memory to the West. For reason is cold, static, and objective; sentiment is warm, dynamic, and subjective; imagination is active and creative; memory is passive and conservative.

To return to the quaternity of ages apportioned to the cardinal points, I shall add that, astrologically speaking, the cycle of the signs of the zodiac begins in the spring with childhood, and ends in winter with old age. Be that as it may, the fact that each thing contains several aspects is enough to account for the divergences of perspective.

5

Man is endowed with a speculative intelligence and a practical intelligence; he is likewise endowed with a spiritual will and a moral will.

The speculative intelligence is necessarily prolonged in and by the spiritual will; the Truth requires a Path.

On the other hand, the practical intelligence and the moral will must be conformable with both the spiritual will and the speculative intelligence, for man is *a priori* a homogeneous being; all the same, anomaly is a possibility with fallen man. Thus, the practical sense may be more or less underdeveloped, which implies a certain lack of sense of proportion; the moral sense, for its part, may be perverted and consequently incompatible with the spiritual life. A lack of practical intelligence—not rare with certain contemplatives—is a relative inconvenience, but not a vice; it may have outward causes, just as it may be the psychological price of a highly developed contemplativity. A lack of moral sensitivity, on the contrary, has not the benefit of any compensating quality, especially as it always implies elements of selfishness, pride, and hypocrisy; there are excuses for weakness, but not for ugliness. Be that as it may, faults of soul—be they major or minor—are curable, for where there is a will, there is a way; and nothing contingent can withstand the rays of the Absolute.

6

We should not be astonished if we notice defects of character, or even vices in a person whose parents are normal or virtuous, for if there were saints whose parents were bad people, the reverse must also be possible, namely that there be bad people whose parents were saints. A person's traits of character have two possible sources: either the individual substance—the origin of which no one knows—or heredity; when a character cannot be explained by heredity, then this means that it is entirely specific to the individual. For a child is not just the product of his parents; he contains something new that derives from himself, otherwise there would never be exceptional men, and otherwise a quality or a defect would always belong to the entire paternal or maternal line, all the way up to the ancestors and up to Cain and Abel. The core of the problem, metaphysically speaking, is All-Possibility; evil cannot not exist since the world is not God; "for it must needs be that offences come", although there is also the parable of the prodigal son. All that we can do in such cases is to pray for the person who has gone astray; this is what Saint Monica did, the mother of Saint Augustine; you could also pray for your grandchildren.

What matters for us is to practice resignation on the one hand and trust on the other hand: resignation to the Will of God and trust in His Mercy.

7

It makes no sense to believe in the devil and then each time, when he appears—most often exploiting a specific situation—to deny that he is involved. One must also keep in mind the fact that there are people who secretly harbor a grave fault which they cover with brilliant bookish knowledge or with a more or less unconscious hypocrisy until the fault, which had been suppressed in a corner, breaks out because it had not been dissolved by humility but was instead gilded with pride; it then breaks out all the more crudely—because it draped itself with holiness instead of just worldliness. The Prophet already spoke about this, and Christian mystics also had much to say about this. Everything depends finally on whether virtue or vice resides in a person's outer being or in his core. Sometimes a weakness can suddenly erupt in a good person but it then exhausts itself, so that this person becomes even better thereby; one must in any case be very prudent in judging the faults of others, and ruthless in judging one's own shortcomings. Moreover, virtue with bitterness is always worthless; bitterness amounts to spiritual suicide. There is a great danger in this for an aging person: he too easily makes others responsible for the disappointments of his youth and then due to his own bitterness falls into even greater errors. Human nature is simply what it is, and no young person can know all of its possibilities. The aging and disappointed man then tends too easily, and falsely, to make sweeping generalizations based on the mistakes of his experiences and, in so doing, he forgets that the experiences one has of human nature do not encompass the whole of man—that the soul of the noble person remains always unexplored virgin territory, for man is indeed able to carry everything within himself, earth and God. Apart from this, one often overlooks that we ourselves disappoint others, because it is human nature to be largely oblivious to one's own faults.

8

Relationships with God: 1. the purely metaphysical, through intellection; 2. the purely human, through faith and the feeling soul; and 3. relationship with God through recourse to the Logos—to a celestial human being. While this third type of relationship, like the second, has its point of departure in the human being as such, it does not imply any intrinsic limitation; but, as just mentioned, the encounter with the divine comes here through the *Avatāra*. The names of Shankara, David, and Honen correspond respectively to these three types of relationship with God; or *Paramātmā*; *Adonai*; Amida.

Thus, firstly a purely metaphysical relationship with the divine, through intellection; secondly, a purely human relationship with God, either direct, or indirect through the mediation of a God-man. On the one hand the purely intellectual and the human relationship are distinct from one another, so that they exist side by side; yet on the other hand they can combine, since in fact metaphysical knowledge has an influence on the human dimension. But this lies in the nature of things and can never depend on an artificial intention.

It could also be said: we face the supra-personal Divinity as pure Intellect; the personal God we face as a human being; and the God-man—and I am thinking in particular of the Holy Virgin here—we face as a child. Now while on the one hand these three relationships are separate, on the other hand they cannot be exclusively distinct.

And likewise: if the supra-personal Divinity, the personal God, and *a fortiori* the God-man are distinct from one another, it must nevertheless be said that at the same time they necessarily touch each other, in the sense that the God-man is the door to God, and through this in a certain manner also the door to Beyond-Being; indeed it can also be said: God and His Name are one. Saint Bernardino of Siena wrote: "All that God has created for the salvation of the world is concealed in the Name of Jesus: the whole of the Bible, from Genesis to the last book." And again: "The Name of Jesus is as worthy of praise as God Himself."

When an adherent of *Advaita Vedānta* utters the word *Ātmā* or *Brahma*, he has said everything; *Īshvara* and the *Avatāra* are in a certain way included. When a Jewish or Islamic follower of Abraham says "God", then he has said everything; the supra-personal content is in principle included; in principle, but obviously not always in fact. And similarly: when a Christian says "Christ", then he has said everything; all of theology and metaphysics is included—the latter in principle and the former in fact.

9

Three spiritual beacons for me are Shankara, Honen, and David: Shankara for metaphysics; Honen for the invocation; and David for prayer. David and Shankara are both prophets within a pre-existing religion, thus they are not founders of a religion, but follow immediately afterwards as luminaries of a first degree of magnitude; Honen is not situated completely on the same level, he is nonetheless a mighty figure owing to his all-encompassing doctrine and its decisive influence, both of which are effects of his holiness.

10

Shankarian Vedantism marked the inauguration of a millennium of intellectual and spiritual flowering; to speak of Hindu wisdom is to speak of Shankarcharya. It was therefore a prospective work, not a retrospective one; it was an opening, not a testament. In short, on the plane of intrinsic metaphysics—not that of the "science of religions"—Shankara was one of the greatest masters that ever lived; his scope was so to speak "prophetic" or "apostolic"; he was, on his plane, as infallible as the *Upanishads*.

11

It occurs to me that, even in India, *bhakti* is often confused with dualistic, anti-advaitist, and thus anti-metaphysical, bhaktism, as if *bhakti* as a spiritual attitude were the equivalent of the limited theology of classical bhaktism, which is based on the *Bhagavata Purāna*. For the love of God of such a one as Shankaracharya—who also spoke of *bhakti*, if only because it is mentioned in the *Bhagavad Gītā* and other sacred texts that are binding for advaitins—is completely independent of any limiting theory. One can love God without believing that *Advaita Vedānta* is false, or that the *māyā*-dependent distinction between *jivātmā* and *Paramātmā* is absolute.

12

Patience and Trust: these are the poles of the soul's equilibrium in the spiritual life: this means two things, namely: firstly, that it is a question here of virtues which are not only natural but spiritual; and secondly that, given this fact, virtues are determined by the spiritual element, Truth on the one hand and Faith on the other hand. This is to say: the sufficient reason of spiritual Patience and spiritual Trust is, on the one hand, the Reality of God and, on the other hand, our Faith in God. This Patience and this Trust are nourished by Truth and Faith.

Natural patience and natural trust are determined, not by the spiritual element, but by the worldly instinct of self-preservation; in these qualities, man remains on his own natural level, he does not surpass himself. On the contrary, each spiritual virtue in a way denotes a victory over earthly nature, thus a victory over ourselves.

Truth and Faith, Thought and Being: this is the vertical dimension. Patience and Trust, Resignation and Fervor: this is the horizontal dimension. To Patience is joined Abstention; he who is patient for God must also abstain from what is spiritually harmful. And to Trust is joined Activity; he who has trust in God must also accomplish what is spiritually useful.

In a strictly principial sense, one may say: Truth and Faith; everything is to be found therein. In referring to the soul one may say: Patience and Trust; everything is to be found therein. And concerning the means, one could say: Abstention and Activity; everything is to be found therein.

13

One of the part-human, part-divine phenomena that has fascinated me ever since my childhood is the *mudrā*; the one in which the hand is vertical, the thumb holding the middle finger so that they form a circle, the ring finger being half inclined, the other two fingers remaining nearly vertical; in short, this *mudrā*-synthesis which seems to present a pearl, a jewel, a *chintāmani*, an elixir; a *mudrā* that teaches and communicates, not through a word, obviously, but through a divine or nirvanic gesture, precisely. A gesture that seems to extract—or to have extracted—what is the most precious, the most directly salvific, from a complex Message; which brings to mind that other *mudrā*, what for the Buddha was the "Flower Sermon".

14

As for the translation of *Rahīm*, one must absolutely find something other than "utterly Merciful", for Arabic superlativism cannot be introduced into European languages in this manner. "Utterly" has the same Germanic root as the German word *äußerst*; when joined with the idea of Mercy, it gives the impression of an excess and of sentimentalism, or of logical unintelligibility; Mercy is inexhaustible, certainly, but it does not prevent the contrary aspect of Rigor; a European expression should be found which, if not exactly adequate, is at least symbolically sufficient, and it should avoid any impression of pure exaggeration. That was in fact the intention of the word "ever". Since "Infinitely Good" was used for *Rahmān*, could not "Inexhaustibly Merciful" be used for *Rahīm*? This is what "Ever Merciful" conveys well, it seems to me; so there is no need to replace it with something else. For the idea is that God can bring about modalities of Mercy even there where man can no longer conceive of them; this is difficult to express in a few words.

15

As I have very rigorous ideas about poetic art, I allow poems to be translated in only two ways: either a literal, word-for-word translation, thus in prose but respecting the lines of the original, or else the poem is translated by strictly applying to it the rules of metrics or of prosody, in which case the translation is inevitably freer, but then it must be a work of art. A third possibility is rhythmic prose, but then it must be truly rhythmic and not merely fitful.

16

Modern-minded people will say that modern civilization entails many improvements, and that the old Indian ways, or every traditional way of life, entail too many evils. But this type of reasoning makes no sense, for what counts are the tendencies of a civilization; a civilization must be considered as a whole and not judged by its parts. In other words: if we consider the old Indian civilization as a whole, we see that its principles and its fundamental tendencies were good and that good things prevail over the evil ones; but if we consider the modern world as a whole, we see that its principles and fundamental tendencies are false—in spite of certain partial improvements—and that the evil things prevail over the good ones. In fact, the ancient Indian was—in spite of all his mistakes—a spiritual man; he was not perfect, but he was more so than most Indians and whites of today; and certainly he could attain perfection on his own cultural ground. The criterion of man or of a world is always the reliance on—and the direction towards—the Truth, the Unseen, the Great Mystery.

17

The "sentimental" or "romantic" character of a type of literature about Indians has an honorable explanation, firstly because of the awareness of the wrongs done to the Indians, and secondly because of the awareness of their moral and aesthetic values, as well as others; but no writer who supposedly "idealized" the Indians ever thought they were without faults; in any case, the point of view of these authors is something that is so innocuous that it has never constituted an obstacle to the study of the red race. Nothing is more vexing than the opposite viewpoint according to which only the small and banal man is the real man.

At all events, "the Indians as they really are" are only rarely the Indians as they are in their substance and as they were still at the beginning of the twentieth century; firstly because everything has been done to transform the Indians into cowboys, and then because one wants to attribute to the "authentic Indian" the cowboyism that has been inflicted on him. The aristocratic and more or less primordial simplicity of the Indian is not at all the same thing as the simplifying and democratic mindset of the average American; to be simple and natural is not to be mentally a barbarian. I draw these remarks from my own experiences.

18

In speaking of Indian dress, I have in mind the archetypal intention—the "idea" it projects through its formal language into the human world—and not the level this intention takes on or is subjected to *de facto* in the awareness of a given majority.

The forms bespeaking an ethnic genius, hence those that are more or less "revealed", are always greater than the average level of those who express it; I have in mind here the profound and spiritual intention of these forms. Be that as it may, and from an altogether elementary point of view, I will say that the Indian genius, and therefore the general costume that manifests it, is at the opposite end of weakness towards oneself and of moral small-mindedness; when one wears an Indian dress, one is ashamed to entertain petty psychological problems.

19

Since I have spoken of dress and of its moral and spiritual requirements, I must add some reflections concerning nudity—which is sacral by definition—when considered according to the same relationship. For here too, "*noblesse oblige*": given that the human body—like man himself—is "made in the image of God", it manifests the universal qualities and therefore all of the virtues; it is essentially vertical and integral, which amounts to saying that it is essentially noble. What is the most outward expresses what is the most inward—this is why Lalla Yogishvari, having realized the Center, danced naked—so that the body reminds man of the heavenly Norm and of the earthly Law. "Extremes meet."

20

The Indian perspective entails first of all reading the primordial teaching in the phenomena of nature—each one reads what he understands—and the experience of nature as being sacred, as the primordial homeland everywhere filled with the Great Spirit and its manifestations; and this awareness gives the American Indian his dignity made of veneration for nature and self-domination; it accounts also for the unique grandeur of his richly accented artistic appearance, in which eagle and sun harmonize and which belongs to the realm of the archetypes, of divine primordial models.

21

The two constitutive elements of the Path are the doctrine and the method. When the Path is reduced to these two poles, all the other possible elements—moral quality, traditional framework, congenial ambience—are included in the method, even though the method, in the most direct sense of the word, consists of concentration, invocation, the Remembrance of God.

But it can also be said that the Path comprises three elements: doctrine, method, and virtue. In other words: comprehension, concentration, and conformity. Or that it comprises four elements, by adding the traditional framework, hence the religion; or five elements, by adding the congenial ambience, hence art and craftsmanship, which are also part of man.

In a traditional civilization, the question of the congenial ambience—dress and habitation—poses no problem; every formal element is a gift of Heaven and thus constitutes a preexistent basis. In the modern world on the contrary, this basis practically no longer exists; the individual must consequently be aware of the problem and keep an eye on the formal integrity of his ambience, in order to avoid as far as possible the presence of forms that are contrary to the truth, the path, and virtue; hence the *barakah*.

Prior to dress there was the naked body; and prior to habitation there was virgin nature. Thus dress must express or prolong the sacred character, the nobleness, and the beauty of the body, as habitation must express or prolong the sacred character, the nobleness, and the beauty of virgin nature; and the same holds true for ornaments and utensils. In no case should the elements that are part of our ambience—according to the meaning we have given to this word—be contrary to the theophanic dignity of our body and of surrounding nature; and nothing in our bodily appearance ought to be rendered contrary to the creative intention of God.

Doubtless one can be perfect, or tend towards perfection, in any formal context; but one may not choose just any formal context in view of perfection. One may not renounce God on account of a spiritually unfavorable condition imposed upon us by the world, nor may one deliberately opt for an unfavorable condition while sincerely desiring God; in other words, one must not accept such a condition when it can be avoided. One may remember God in every circumstance, but one may not choose every circumstance with the intention of remembering God.

Within the congenial ambience, there is a choice possible between simplicity and sumptuousness, or between poverty and richness; clearly, simplicity comes first, but sumptuousness—which in this case is not luxury—nonetheless has an aesthetic, liturgical, or social justification depending upon the spiritual realities or traditional function which one has the right or duty of manifesting; or also, in certain cases, depending upon the legitimate needs of a given soul in given circumstances.

It should be noted that errors and deviations can be produced even in the framework of traditional art, just as manifestations of formal correctness can be produced even in a deviated world; which proves nothing either against tradition or in favor of anti-tradition.

The Prophet said: "God is beautiful and He loveth beauty." And Plato: "Beauty is the splendor of the true."

22

Man's situation consists in seeing God from the starting-point of the world. Now to see God from the starting-point of the world, is to see the world from the starting-point of God. To see God from the starting-point of the world is to see God as Lord, as Principle which determines everything; to see the world from the starting-point of God is to see the world as a unity which is contingent and transitory. Profane man sees about him things, persons, events, but not the ontological and eschatological veil into which they are woven; he does not see the world from a distance, as one views a landscape from the height of a mountain; he sees contents, but not the container. "He does not see the forest for the trees" (*vor Baumen den Wald nicht sehen*): under the hypnosis of appearances he sees neither the *Māyā* by and in which he exists, nor the *Samsāra* within which his destiny is played-out. The spiritual man, on the contrary, since he never loses sight of the Principle, cannot, in perceiving things, lose sight of what they are with regard to the Principle that determines them. The spiritual man is consciously situated between God and the world, and that is why he is *pontifex* or *khalīfah*; he must link the world to God while representing God in the world. He must introduce God into the world and bring the world—his soul—back to God.

To see the world from the starting-point of God is not only to see its contingency and its finitude, but also to see, within things, its message of Absoluteness and Infinitude; for if the world on the one hand veils God, it also communicates the Archetypes, the Qualities, the Mysteries, by means of symbols and beauties; by means also of privations and contrasts.

To see God from the starting-point of the world is to see the world from the starting-point of God. But there is in man a region—the Heart-Intellect—which is not in the world, and in which God knows Himself; in an inversely analogous way, there is a plane upon which man perceives things in themselves and independently of their ontological and eschatological context. Quite clearly, these perspectives are parallel and do not contradict each other.

To see God from the starting-point of the world, as transcendent Lord; but to know Him also through Himself, as immanent Self. To see the world from the starting-point of God, as impermanent veil; but also to comprehend its messages of Reality and of Eternity. To see in God the roots of things, is to see in the world the reflections of God.

EDITOR'S NOTES

Numbers in bold indicate pages in the text for which the following citations and explanations are provided.

Foreword

xi: Jalal ad-Din *Rumi* (1207-73) was one of the greatest Sufi mystics and poets, and the founder of the Mevlevi order.

"*One thing needful*": "One thing is needful: and Mary hath chosen that good part, which shall not be taken from her" (Luke 10:42).

The *Duke of Orléans*, Louis Philippe I (1773-1850), became King of France in 1830.

To Have a Center

3: "And Jesus knew their thoughts and said unto them, Every kingdom divided against itself is brought to desolation; and every city or *house divided against itself* shall not stand" (Matt. 12:25).

5: Abu Hamid Muhammad al-*Ghazzali* (c. 1058-1111) was an Islamic jurist, theologian, and mystic.

Christ could say that what is impossible for man is always possible for God: "And he said, the things which are impossible with men are possible with God" (Luke 18:12).

Note 5: *The Hindu system* of caste is discussed more fully in the author's essay, "The Meaning of Caste", in *Language of the Self* (Bloomington, IN: World Wisdom, 1999), pp. 113-146.

8: *Dante* Alighieri (1265-1321) was the author of *The Divine Comedy*, one of the pinnacles of world literature. Ananda K. Coomaraswamy declared Dante, along with Meister Eckhart (see editor's note for Ch. "Universal Categories", p. 61), to be the "greatest of all Europeans" ("The Vedānta and Western Tradition", in *Coomaraswamy 2: Metaphysics*, ed. Roger Lipsey [Princeton: Princeton University Press, 1977], p. 6).

Virgil (70-19 B.C.) was a Roman poet whose principal works are the *Aeneid*, the *Ecologues*, and the *Georgics*.

9: Immanuel *Kant* (1724-1804), a German philosopher influenced by Enlightenment thinkers, sought a rational basis for morality in the principle of "the categorical imperative".

Jean-Jacques *Rousseau* (1712-78) was a French philosopher and writer, associated with the ideas of "natural goodness" and the "noble savage".

Friedrich *Nietzsche* (1844-1900), a German writer and philosopher, rejected Christian and humanistic ethical systems in his *adventurous amoralism.*

Voltaire (1694-1778), the pseudonym of François-Marie Arouet, was the best known of the Enlightenment *philosophes.* A deist, he was an implacable critic of organized religion in satirical works such as *Candide.*

Note 10: Antonio *Canova* (1757-1822) was a neoclassical Venetian sculptor, best known for his marble nudes.

Jean-Auguste-Dominique *Ingres* (1780-1867) was a neoclassical French painter.

10: Ludwig van *Beethoven* (1770-1827) was a German composer who had a profound influence on the development of European music.

Note 13: *Ramakrishna* (1834-86), a devotee of the Goddess Kali, was one of the greatest Hindu saints of modern times, well-known for frequently falling into ecstatic trance (*samādhi*).

Note 14: Johann Sebastian *Bach* (1685-1750) was the pre-eminent composer of the baroque period.

Wolfgang Amadeus *Mozart* (1756-91) was the greatest composer and musician of his era.

11: Wilhelm Richard *Wagner* (1813-83) was a German composer known mainly for his grandiose operas.

Auguste *Rodin* (1840-1917) is widely regarded as the father of modern sculpture.

Michelangelo di Lodovico Buonarroti (1475-1564) painted the frescoes on the ceiling of the Sistine Chapel in the Vatican Palace, as well as the *Last Judgment.*

Donatello (1386-1466), or Donato di Niccolò di Betto Bardi, a sculptor, and Benvenuto *Cellini* (1500-71), a goldsmith, painter, and sculptor, were artists of the Italian Renaissance.

Note 16: Antoine *Bourdelle* (1861-1929) was a French sculptor, painter, and teacher.

Aristide *Maillol* (1861-1944) was a French sculptor, painter, printmaker, and designer.

12: *The Age of Philosophy* refers to the rationalist and humanistic works of the Enlightenment philosophers of the late seventeenth and eighteenth century.

The French *Revolution* of 1789-99 destroyed the *Ancien Régime.*

Charlemagne (c. 742-814) was the first Emperor of the Holy Roman Empire.

Saint Louis (1214-70) was the King of France from 1226 until his death.

Thus Spoke Zarathustra*: A Book for All and None* (1883-85), was a major work of Friedrich *Nietzsche.*

13: *Napoleon* Bonaparte (1769-1821) was a French military and political leader who became Emperor of the French from 1804-14.

Johann Wolfgang von *Goethe* (1749-1832) was a German poet, novelist, and playwright. In his work *Faust*, published in two parts, in 1808 and posthumously in 1832, he reworked the German legend about the scholar who sells his soul to Mephistopheles (the Devil) in exchange for boundless knowledge and power.

The Jewish philosopher Baruch *Spinoza* (1632-77), placed under a ban by his co-religionists because of his alleged pantheism, construed the existence of the Divine in such a way as to equate its reality with that of nature, God being the universal substance of which all things are made.

Walter von der Vogelweide (1170-c. 1230) was a medieval lyric poet and musician.

Note 18: Basing itself on the evidence of nature, *eighteenth century deism* accepted the existence of a creator God, but rejected Revelation, authority, and institutional religion.

Note 19: Johann Friedrich von *Schiller* (1759-1805) was a German poet, philosopher, and historian, who was also a friend of Goethe.

14: Honoré *Balzac* (1799-1850) was a French playwright and novelist, best known for a series of stories and novels collectively called *La Comédie humaine.*

Charles *Dickens* (1812-70) was a prolific and highly popular English novelist.

Leo *Tolstoy* (1828-1910), a Russian writer of such works as *War and Peace* and *Anna Karenina*, was widely considered to be one of the world's greatest novelists.

Fyodor *Dostoevsky* (1821-81) was the Russian author of such novels as *Crime and Punishment* and *The Brothers Karamazov.*

Oscar Wilde (1854-1900), an Irish writer best known for his witty plays and epigrams, was imprisoned in *Reading Gaol* in 1897 after being convicted on homosexual charges of "gross indecency". After his release in 1898 he wrote the long poem, "The Ballad of Reading Gaol".

Note 20: Miguel de *Cervantes* Saavedra (1547-1616) was a Spanish poet, novelist, and playwright, and the author of *Don Quixote.*

William *Shakespeare* (1564-1616) was a playwright, poet, and actor, and is widely regarded as the greatest writer in the English language.

Pedro *Calderón* de la Barca (1600-81) was a Spanish writer, soldier, and priest, and the greatest dramatist of the "Golden Age" of Spanish theater.

The tragedies of Antiquity refers to the works of the great Greek dramatists Aeschylus (c. 525-456 B.C.), Sophocles (c. 496-406 B.C.), and Euripides (c. 480-406 B.C.).

Note 22: Hans Christian *Andersen* (1805-75), a prolific Danish writer in many genres, is best known for his fairy tales.

15: *Lenau* was the *nom-de-plume* of the Austrian poet, Nicholas Franz Niembsch von Strehlenau (1820-50).

Dante's *Vita Nuova* ("The New Life") is a *prosimetrum*, a work in both prose and verse, which celebrates his love for the young woman Beatrice.

Orpheus is the mythical archetype of the inspired singer; in classical mythology he played divine music in an attempt to retrieve his wife, Eurydice, from the underworld.

In classical mythology, *sirens* were beautiful and seductive creatures who lured sailors into shipwreck and death through their enchanting music.

Vincent *Van Gogh* (1853-90) was a Dutch post-impressionist painter who achieved little recognition during his lifetime but is now widely regarded as one of the greatest painters of his period.

Paul *Gaugin* (1848-1903) was a French post-impressionist whose work, like that of Van Gogh, was not widely recognized until after his death.

Note 24: *Francis of Sales* (1567-1622) was a Bishop of Geneva and the author of several spiritual treatises. He was canonized in 1665 and declared a Doctor of the Church in 1877.

Hindu tradition tells of the *avatāra Krishna* enthralling the adoring *gopīs* or cowherd girls of Vrindavan with the music of his *flute.*

16: Georges *Bizet* (1838-75) was a French composer in the Romantic vein, best known for his opera *Carmen.*

Henrik *Ibsen* (1828-1906) was an influential Norwegian playwright whose works dealt with controversial subjects and themes.

August *Strindberg* (1849-1912) was a prolific and iconoclastic Swedish writer, prominent in the European *avant-garde.*

"*After me the flood*" (in French, "Après moi, le deluge"), is a phrase attributed to Louis XV (1710-74), King of France and Navarre.

In *Goethe's* "The *Sorcerer's Apprentice*", the dilettante protagonist dabbles with magical powers that he is subsequently unable to control.

Victor Hugo (1802-55), a poet, novelist, and dramatist, was one of the most successful French writers of his day, best known for his works *Les Misérables* and *The Hunchback of Notre-Dame.*

17: The *Orientales* was a collection of poems by Victor Hugo, inspired by the Greek War of Independence.

18: *Maine de Biran* (1766-1824) was a French statesman and empiricist philosopher who in his later years became interested in the interior life of the spirit.

Louis-Claude de *Saint-Martin* (1743-1803) was a visionary French philosopher influenced by the mystical writings of Jakob Boehme (1575-1624) and Emanuel Swedenborg (1688-1772).

Franz von *Baader* (1765-1841) was a German Catholic philosopher and theologian, influenced by the writings of Meister Eckhart, Paracelsus (see editor's note for Ch. "Degrees and Dimensions of Theism", p. 90, Note 3), and Jakob Boehme.

Friedrich Wilhelm Joseph *Schelling* (1775-1854) was a German idealist philosopher.

The Hegelian dialectic refers to the philosophical method of G.W.F. Hegel (1770-1831), the foremost figure in German idealism, who posited that a thesis is opposed by an antithesis, which in turn is resolved by a synthesis.

Note 26: *Liberal theologians* embraced modern scientism—notably the new rationalist and empiricist methodologies of Biblical "criticism"—in order to reinterpret religion and scripture. Elsewhere the author remarks that "Modern exegesis is only a caricature of ancient hermeneutics, if indeed there remains any relationship between them; it consists above all in giving doubts and prejudices the status of dogmas: according to these prejudices, it is 'impossible' that a book should be prior to a certain date or that a scribe should have copied a book, even a sacred one, without altering it; quite improper conclusions are drawn from the smallest facts, and the most disproportionate deductions and inductions are allowed even though all the positive data are contrary to these false principles" (Frithjof Schuon, *Gnosis: Divine Wisdom: A New Translation with Selected Letters*, ed. James S. Cutsinger [Bloomington, IN: World Wisdom, 2006], p. 11n); "In order to understand the nature of the Bible and its meaning, it is essential to have recourse to the ideas of both symbolism and revelation; without an exact and, in the measure necessary, sufficiently profound understanding of these key ideas, the approach to the Bible remains hazardous and risks engendering grave doctrinal, psychological, and historical errors" (Frithjof Schuon, *Light on the Ancient Worlds: A New Translation with Selected Letters*, ed. Deborah Casey [Bloomington, IN: World Wisdom, 2006], p. 115).

Scholasticism was the system of theology and philosophy taught in medieval European universities, based on Aristotelian logic and the writings of the early Church Fathers.

19: René *Descartes* (1596-1650) propounded a philosophical method based upon the systematic doubting of everything except one's own self-consciousness, as summed up in the Latin phrase *cogito ergo sum* ("I think; therefore I am").

Note 28: *Léon Bloy* (1846-1917) was a French writer who converted to

Roman Catholicism at the age of eighteen and became a passionate but largely ineffective advocate for religious faith.

20: Jean *Racine* (1639-99) and Pierre *Corneille* (1606-84) were great French dramatists of the seventeenth century.

Molière was the stage name of Jean-Baptiste Poquelin (1622-73), an actor and dramatist whose plays are widely considered to be masterpieces of comedy.

Blaise *Pascal* (1623-62) was a French philosopher, mathematician, and scientist.

Jean de *La Fontaine* (1621-95) was a French poet and writer of fables.

Charles *Perrault* (1628-1703) pioneered the new literary genre of fairy tales. Many of his stories were later rewritten by the Brothers Grimm.

Louise Labé (c. 1520-1566), a French poet of the Renaissance period, wrote twenty-four sonnets influenced by Neoplatonism and by Petrarch.

Francesco Petrarca, or *Petrarch* (1304-74), was a humanist scholar and poet of the Italian Renaissance.

Rainer Maria *Rilke* (1875-1926) was a Bohemian-Austrian writer whose lyric poetry contains a distinctively mystical strain.

Aristotle (384-322 B.C.) was a pupil of Plato (see editor's note for Ch. "The Primacy of Intellection", p. 50), and one of the greatest philosophers of antiquity.

21: Publius Cornelius *Tacitus* (c. 56-c. 117) was a member of the Roman Senate and a historian of the Roman Empire. His *De origine et situ Germanorum* ("The Origin and Location of the Germans") describes in great detail the German peoples at the end of the first century A.D.

22: For further commentary on *the mystery of Eve* see the author's "The Primordial Tree", in *Esoterism as Principle and as Way* (London: Perennial Books, 1981), pp. 79-89; on *the mystery of Mary* see the author's "Christic and Virginal Mysteries", in *Gnosis: Divine Wisdom*, pp. 119-124.

Albert *Einstein* (1879-1955) was a German physicist and mathematician who developed the general theory of relativity.

23: Henry de *Montherlant* (1895-1972) was a French essayist, novelist, and dramatist.

Note 33: Heinrich *Heine* (1797-1856) was a German poet, journalist, and literary critic.

24: *Snow White* and *Sleeping Beauty* were German fairy tales popularized by the Brothers Grimm in the early nineteenth century.

25: Abraham *Lincoln* (1809-65) was the sixteenth president of the United States.

Note 35: *Chiang Kai-shek* (1887-1975) was an anti-communist Chinese military and political leader.

26: Mohandas K. *Gandhi* (1869-1948) was the leader of the anti-British Indian independence movement and an advocate of non-violent civil disobedience.

27: Note 38: *Hinmaton-Yalatkit* ("*Chief Joseph*") (1840-1904) was a warrior and leader of the Nez Percé Indians who, under attack by the U.S. Army, fled into Canada.

Tecumseh (1768-1813) was a chief of the Shawnee tribe of American Indians and the leader of "Tecumseh's Confederacy" against the United States in the War of 1812.

Tammany or Tamanend (c. 1625-1701), a chief of one of the Delaware tribes, played a central role in establishing peaceful relations with the English settlers in Pennsylvania.

30: *Fra Angelico* (1387-1455) was a Dominican friar of the monastery of Fiesole, Italy, as well as a famous painter of the Florentine School.

To build his house either on sand or on a rock: "Therefore whosoever heareth these sayings of mine, and doeth them, I will liken him unto a wise man, which built his house upon a rock: And the rain descended, and the floods came, and the winds blew, and beat upon that house; and it fell not: for it was founded upon a rock. And every one that heareth these sayings of mine, and doeth them not, shall be likened unto a foolish man, which built his house upon the sand: And the rain descended, and the floods came, and the winds blew, and beat upon that house; and it fell: and great was the fall of it" (Matt. 7:24-27).

Overview of Anthropology

34: "*What is impossible for man, is possible for God*": "With men this is impossible; but with God all things are possible" (Matt. 19:26).

35: Note 3: For *Lincoln* see editor's note for Ch. "To Have a Center", p. 25.

George *Washington* (1732-99) was one of the founding fathers of the United States and its first president.

For *Napoleon* see editor's note for Ch. "To Have a Center", p. 13.

For *Beethoven* see editor's note for Ch. "To Have a Center", p. 10.

Emir Abd el-Kader al-Jazairi (1808-83) was a Muslim leader, scholar, and mystic who led the Algerian rebellion against the French colonizers.

For *Ramakrishna* see editor's note for Ch. "To Have a Center", p. 10.

Ramana Maharshi (1879-1950), was an exponent of *Advaita Vedānta* and one of the greatest sages of the modern era. Elsewhere the author has written of him: "In Sri Ramana Maharshi one meets ancient and eternal India again. Vedantic truth—that of the *Upanishads*—is reduced to its simplest expression. . . . In these latter days Sri Ramana was at it were the incarnation of what is primordial and incorruptible in India" (*Spiritual Perspectives and Human Facts: A New Translation with Selected Letters*, ed. James S. Cutsinger [Bloomington, IN: World Wisdom, 2007], p. 129).

36: Note 4: Houston Stewart *Chamberlain* (1855-1927), an Englishman who later became a German citizen, was the author of *The Foundations of the Nineteenth Century* in which he developed his racial theory about the superiority of the Aryans.

Arthur de *Gobineau* (1816-82) was a French aristocrat and writer who acclaimed Aryans as the "Master Race" in *An Essay on the Inequality of the Human Races.* He was one of the earliest exponents of what came to be called "scientific racism", that is, racial theories purportedly based on scientific evidence.

Hans *Günther* (1891-1968), a German racial theorist and eugenicist, was a major influence on Nazi racial ideology.

37: Note 5: *Don Quixote* is the eponymous hero of the famous work by Cervantes (see editor's note for Ch. "To Have a Center", p. 14); *Sancho Panza* is Don Quixote's squire.

39: For *Gnosticism* and the term "gnosis", see the essay "Gnosis Is Not Just Anything" in the present volume.

40: *Transformist evolutionism*, such as that proposed by Charles Darwin (1809-82), supposes that one species can transform into another by a process of random mutation.

"Behold, there appeared a *chariot of fire*, and horses of fire, and parted them both asunder; and *Elijah* went up by a whirlwind into heaven" (2 Kings 2:11).

The "cloud" that enveloped Christ during his ascension: "And when he had spoken these things, while they beheld, he [Christ] was taken up; and a cloud received him out of their sight" (Acts 1:9).

Our conception of the origin of mankind is based on the doctrine of the projection of the archetypes ab intra: elsewhere the author remarks: "The origin of a creature is not a material substance, it is a perfect and non-material archetype: perfect, therefore without any need of a transformative evolution; non-material, therefore having its origin in the Spirit, not in matter" (Frithjof Schuon, *From the Divine to the Human: A New Translation with Selected Letters*, ed. Patrick Laude [Bloomington, IN: World Wisdom, 2013], p. 14).

Our position is that of classical emanationism—in the Neoplatonic or gnostic sense of the term—which avoids the pitfall of anthropomorphism while agreeing with the theological conception of creatio ex nihilo: elsewhere the author clarifies the meanings of *classical emanationism* and *creatio ex nihilo* further: "We understand the term 'emanation' in the Platonic sense: the starting point remains transcendent, hence unaffected, whereas in deist or naturalist emanationism the cause pertains to the same ontological order as the effect" (Frithjof Schuon, *Roots of the Human Condition* [Bloomington, IN: World Wisdom, 1991], p. 5n); "When one speaks traditionally of *creatio ex nihilo*, what is meant, on the one hand, is that creatures do not derive from a pre-existing matter and, on the other, that the 'incarnation' of possibilities cannot in any way affect the immutable Plenitude of the Principle" (Frithjof Schuon, *From the Divine to the Human*, p. 14).

Intelligence and Character

43: *Beauty is the splendor of the true*, a fundamental axiom of the author's perspective, is attributed to *Plato* (see editor's note for Ch. "The Primacy of Intellection", p. 50).

"*Love one's neighbor as oneself*": "Thou shalt love thy neighbor as thyself" (Matt. 19:19, Matt. 22:39, Mark 12:31; cf. Luke 10:27).

44: *The Bible speaks of "mockers"*: "Are there not mockers with me? and doth not mine eye continue in their provocation?" (Job 17:2); "With hypocritical mockers in feasts, they gnashed upon me with their teeth (Psalms 35:16); "I sat not in the assembly of the mockers, nor rejoiced; I sat alone because of thy hand: for thou hast filled me with indignation" (Jer. 15:17); "And when they had platted a crown of thorns, they put it upon his head, and a reed in his right hand: and they bowed the knee before him, and mocked him, saying, Hail, King of the Jews! And they spit upon him, and took the reed, and smote him on the head. And after that they had mocked him, they took the robe off from him, and put his own raiment on him, and led him away to crucify him" (Matt. 27:29-31); "And when they heard of the resurrection of the dead, some mocked: and others said, We will hear thee again of this matter" (Acts 17:32).

"*There is no right superior to that of truth*" is a traditional Hindu maxim attributed to the Maharajahs of Benares.

46: "He that loveth not knoweth not God; for *God is love*" (1 John 4:8).

"*God alone is good*": "Why callest thou me good? There is none good but one, that is, God" (Matt. 19:17; Mark 10:18).

The Primacy of Intellection

47: *Augustine* (354-430), Bishop of the North African city of Hippo, was one of the greatest of the Western Church Fathers.

Anselm (c. 1033-1109), Archbishop of Canterbury, formulated his famous *ontological proof* for the existence *of God* in his work, *Proslogion*, arguing that God is "that than which nothing greater can be conceived".

48: "*He who knoweth his soul, knoweth his Lord*" (*hadīth*).

The oracle at Delphi was a prophetic priestess called the Pythia. The saying, "*Know thyself*" (*Gnothi seauton*), was inscribed over the portal to the Temple of Apollo in Delphi.

49: "*The doctrine of Unity is unique*" is a traditional Sufi adage.

Ramanuja (1017-c. 1157) was the pre-eminent exponent of *Vishishta Advaita*, that is, the Hindu *darshana* or perspective of "qualified non-dualism" which foregrounds the personal nature of God.

50: "*Iron age*": in its most representative form, the Hindu doctrine of cosmic cycles divides time qualitatively into *mahāyugas* or "great ages", each comprising four lesser ages (*yugas*) or periods of time, namely, the *Krita-Yuga* (the "golden" age of Western tradition), *Tretā-Yuga* ("silver"), *Dvāpara-Yuga* ("bronze"), and *Kali-Yuga* ("iron"); the latter "marks the end of a great cyclic period of terrestrial humanity" (Frithjof Schuon, *The Transcendent Unity of Religions* [Wheaton, IL: Theosophical Publishing House, 1993], p. xxxiii). One of the hallmarks of the terminal "iron age" is the comparative *absence of metaphysical intellection.*

"*A house divided against itself*": "Every kingdom divided against itself is brought to desolation; and a house divided against a house falleth" (Luke 11:17).

For an extended discussion of what the term *rationalism* properly entails, see the author's "Rationalism Real and Apparent", in *Logic and Transcendence: A New Translation with Selected Letters*, ed. James S. Cutsinger (Bloomington, IN: World Wisdom, 2009), pp. 28-45.

Note 1: for *Aristotle* see editor's note for Ch. "To Have a Center", p. 20.

Plato (c. 427-c. 347 B.C.) was a student of Socrates, teacher of Aristotle, and the greatest of the ancient Greek philosophers. In the *Republic*, Bk. 6 (509d-511e), he carefully distinguished between reason (*dianoia*) and intellection (*noesis*).

51: *Pascal's* (see editor's note for Ch. "To Have a Center", p. 20) *Wager* is to be found in the French philosopher's posthumously published *Pensées* (1669) and posits that there is more to be gained from a belief in God than from atheism even though the truth cannot be decisively established.

Note 2: for *Kant* see editor's note for Ch. "To Have a Center", p. 9.

Gnosis Is Not Just Anything

53: *Spiritualism*, a movement which burgeoned in Europe in the second half of the nineteenth century, preoccupied itself with efforts at communing with the spirits of the dead.

Theosophism refers to a welter of late nineteenth century sects, cults, and organizations which laid claim to a divine wisdom of immemorial origin.

Pseudo-esoterisms refers to *fin-de-siècle* European movements of a purportedly "mystical" and "occult" nature, often bent on reviving a "secret knowledge" from the distant past.

The *Manichean cult* is a dualistic and syncretistic religion that originated in the Persian Empire in the second century A.D. It is based on the heretical Gnostic idea that spirits from a transcendent realm of light have become imprisoned in the darkness of matter and can be liberated from their bondage only by agents sent by the "Father of Light", who in different versions include Zoroaster, the Buddha, the prophets of Israel, Jesus, and the founder of the sect itself, Mani (c. 216-76).

54: The saying, "*Know thyself*" (*Gnothi seauton*), was inscribed over the portal to the *temple* of Apollo *in Delphi.*

"*The kingdom of God is within you*" (Luke 17:21).

55: *Beauty is* "*the splendor of the true*" is an axiom the author attributes to Plato (see editor's note for Ch. "The Primacy of Intellection", p. 50).

The *Asharites* comprised an early school of speculative Islamic theology, based on the teaching of Abu al-Hasan al-Ashari (873-935). For further commentary on Ashari see the author's "The Exo-Esoteric Symbiosis", in *Sufism: Veil and Quintessence: A New Translation with Selected Letters*, ed. James S. Cutsinger (Bloomington, IN: World Wisdom, 2006), pp. 31-33.

Ibn Rushd or Abu al-Walid Muhammad (1126-98), known in the West as Averroes, was an Andalusian polymath and one of the greatest of Islamic philosophers.

For *Ghazzali* see editor's note for Ch. "To Have a Center", p. 5.

56: Note 3: "They cried: Burn him and stand by your gods, if ye will be doing. We [God] said: O *fire, be coolness* and peace for *Abraham*" (*Sūrah* "The Prophets" [21]:68-69).

Universal Categories

59: The *Peripatetic* school of philosophy was founded by *Aristotle* (see editor's note for Ch. "To Have a Center", p. 20) in Athens in c. 335 B.C.; the name of the school is said to derive either from the "columns" (*peripatoi*) of the Lyceum, where the Greek philosopher met with his disciples, or from the Greek word for "wandering" or "walking about" (*peripatetikos*), which Aristotle is said to have done while teaching.

60: For *Augustine* see editor's note for Ch. "The Primacy of Intellection", p. 47.

61: *Meister Eckhart* (c. 1260-1327) was a German Dominican theologian and mystic, regarded by the author as the greatest of Christian metaphysicians and esoterists.

Note 6: On the subject of *evil* and the "*serpent*" *of Paradise* see the author's "The Primordial Tree", in *Esoterism as Principle and as Way* (London: Perennial Books, 1981), pp. 79-89, and "Delineations of Original Sin", in *The Play of Masks* (Bloomington, IN: World Wisdom, 1992), pp. 55-60.

63: In the philosophy of Immanuel Kant (see editor's note for Ch. "To Have a Center", p. 9) the noumenon or "*thing in itself*" (*das Ding an sich*) is distinguished from the "phenomenon" or the thing as it appears to the senses. According to Kant, the "thing in itself" cannot be known directly because of *the inadequacy of cognition.*

64: According to Meister Eckhart, "There is something in the soul that is *uncreated and uncreatable*" (*aliquid est in anima quod est increatum et increabile*), namely the pure *Intellect.*

Cataphatic theology affirms God's positive attributes while *apophatic* theology, or *via negativa* ("negative way"), describes God by negation.

65: Note 8: For *Pascal* see editor's note for Ch. "To Have a Center", p. 20.

Note 9: The author's *Résumé de métaphysique intégrale* (Paris: Le Courrier du Livre, 1985) appeared in English translation as *Survey of Metaphysics and Esoterism* (Bloomington, IN: World Wisdom Books, 1986, 2000).

67: For a fuller discussion of *Pythagorean number* see the author's "Concerning Pythagorean Numbers", in *The Eye of the Heart: Metaphysics, Cosmology, Spiritual Life* (Bloomington, IN: World Wisdom, 1997), pp. 19-26.

68: Note 11: *Wilhelm II* (1859-1941) was the last *German Emperor* and King of Prussia who, during a visit to Corfu, developed a keen interest in *archeology.*

The prophet *Zoroaster* (fl. c. tenth century), also known as Zarathustra, was the founder of the Persian religion of Zoroastrianism.

For *Manicheism* see editor's note for Ch. "Gnosis Is Not Just Anything", p. 53.

71: "*The kingdom of God is within you*" (Luke 17:21).

"*Made in the image of God*": "And God said, Let us make man in our image, after our likeness" (Gen. 1:26).

75: The "*double truth*" *of the Scholastics* (see editor's note for Ch. "To Have a Center", p. 18) distinguished between reason and faith as complementary sources of truth, each being valid within their respective domains. While the Copernican scientific claim that *the earth turns around the sun* was viewed as a lesser truth of reason, the scriptural miracle of the sun standing still when Joshua fought at Jericho (see Josh. 10:12-14) was seen as a greater truth of faith.

76: Note 20: Claudius *Ptolemy* (c. 90-c. 168) was an Alexandrian astronomer, geographer, and poet who proposed a geocentric model of the solar system.

Galileo Galilei (1564-1642), an Italian physicist, mathematician, and astronomer, was tried by the Church for propounding the Copernican theory of heliocentrism as if it were the only way to account for the facts of experience.

77: Moses *Maimonides* (1135-1204), a Jewish rabbi, astronomer, and physician, and one of the most important of the medieval philosophers, is best known for his *Guide of the Perplexed.*

"*Nothing is like unto Him*" (*Sūrah* "Consultation" [42]:11).

"*God is the light of the heavens and of the earth*" (*Sūrah* "Light" [24]:35).

"*God's Hand is above their hands*" (*Sūrah* "Victory" [48]:10).

79: *The purified heart is Elijah's altar upon which the heavenly fire descends*: "And Elijah took twelve stones, according to the number of the tribes of the sons of Jacob, unto whom the word of the Lord came, saying, Israel shall be thy name: And with the stones he built an altar in the name of the Lord. . . . And it came to pass at the time of the offering of the evening sacrifice, that Elijah the prophet came near, and said, Lord God of Abraham, Isaac, and of Israel, let it be known this day that thou art God in Israel, and that I am thy servant, and that I have done all these things at thy word. Hear me, O Lord, hear me, that this people may know that thou art the Lord God, and that thou hast turned their heart back again. Then the fire of the Lord fell, and consumed the burnt sacrifice. . ." (1 Kings 18:31-32, 36-38).

Concerning an Onto-Cosmological Ambiguity

82: *In Semitic monotheism, Satan appears first of all as an evil genius paradoxically in the service of God*: "Now there was a day when the sons of God came to present themselves before the Lord, and Satan came also among them. And the Lord said unto Satan, Whence comest thou? Then Satan answered the

Lord, and said, From going to and fro in the earth, and from walking up and down in it. And the Lord said unto Satan, Hast thou considered my servant Job, that there is none like him in the earth, a perfect and an upright man, one that feareth God, and escheweth evil? Then Satan answered the Lord, and said, . . . put forth thine hand now, and touch all that he hath, and he will curse thee to thy face. And the Lord said unto Satan, Behold, all that he hath is in thy power; only upon himself put not forth thine hand. So Satan went forth from the presence of the Lord" (Job 1:6-9, 11-12); "And (remember) when thy Lord said unto the angels: Lo! I am creating a mortal out of potter's clay of black mud altered. So, when I have made him and have breathed into him of My spirit, do ye fall down, prostrating yourselves unto him. So the angels fell prostrate, all of them together. Save Iblis. He refused to be among the prostrate. He [God] said: O Iblis! What aileth thee that thou art not among the prostrate? He said: Why should I prostrate myself unto a mortal whom Thou hast created out of potter's clay of black mud altered? He said: Then go thou forth from hence, for verily thou art outcast. And lo! the curse shall be upon thee till the Day of Judgment. He said: My Lord! Reprieve me till the day when they are raised. He said: Then lo! thou art of those reprieved. Till an appointed time. He said: My Lord, Because Thou has sent me astray, I verily shall adorn the path of error for them in the earth, and shall mislead them every one. Save such of them as are Thy perfectly devoted slaves. He said: This is a right course incumbent upon Me: Lo! as for My slaves, thou hast no power over any of them save such of the froward as follow thee, And lo! for all such, hell will be the promised place (*Sūrah* "*Al-Hijr*" [15]:28-43).

The Latin phrase *Princeps huius mundi* means "the prince of this world", that is, Satan, and comes from the Vulgate text of John 12:31, 14:30, and 16:11.

God "hardens the heart of Pharaoh": "And the Lord hardened the heart of Pharaoh, and he hearkened not unto them" (Exod. 9:12; cf. Exod. 10:20, 11:10, 14:8).

"*God leads into error*"*—according to the Koran—by turning away from man, not by determining him*: "God confirms those who believe with the firm word, in the present life and in the world to come; and God leads astray the evildoers; and God does what He will" (*Sūrah* "Abraham" [14]:27).

The Koran says more than once that it is not God who wrongs man but that it is man who wrongs himself: "God wronged them not, but they did wrong themselves" (*Sūrah* "Imran" [3]:117); "So God surely wronged them not, but they did wrong themselves" (*Sūrah* "Repentance" [9]:70); "Lo! God wrongeth not mankind in aught; but mankind wrong themselves" (*Sūrah* "Jonah" [10]:44), *passim*.

Note 1: King *Solomon* (r.c. 970-931 B.C.) was the son of David and the builder of the First Temple in Jerusalem. The *Koran* relates that he *had in his service demons to carry out all sorts of tasks*: "And unto Solomon (We gave) . . . certain of the *jinn* [demons] who worked before him by permission of his Lord. And such of them as deviated from Our command, them We caused to taste the punishment of flaming fire. They made for him what he willed: synagogues and statues, basins like wells and boilers built into the ground" (*Sūrah* "Sheba" [34]:12-13).

83: *He* [the devil] *is "made of fire", as the Koran says*: "And We [God] created you, then fashioned you, then told the angels: Fall ye prostrate before Adam! And they fell prostrate, all save Iblis [the devil], who was not of those who make prostration. He [God] said: What hindered thee that thou didst not fall prostrate when I bade thee? (Iblis) said: I am better than him. Thou createdst me of fire while him Thou didst create of mud" (*Sūrah* "The Heights" [7]:11-12).

Shiva is the third god of the Hindu trinity (*trimūrti*), Brahmā being the first and Vishnu the second, and is associated with the powers of generation and destruction.

Note 3: *Mephisto*, or Mephistopheles, is the devil in *Goethe's* tragic play *Faust* (see editor's note for Ch. "To Have a Center", p. 13).

84: *The myth of Lucifer's fall—or the "fall of the angels"*—is recounted in Isa. 14:12-23 and *Sūrah* "The Cow" [2]:34).

The *seal of Solomon* was a ring with magical powers, composed of two superimposed equilateral triangles, one with its apex pointing upward, and the other with its apex pointing downward; the term later came to refer solely to the Star of David.

Note 3: *Kali* is the destructive and transformative manifestation of the Hindu goddess Parvati, consort of Shiva.

85: In Zoroastrianism, *Ahuramazda or Ormuzd* is the Supreme Lord of the universe, and *Angra Mainyu or Ahriman* is an evil spirit corresponding to Satan in the Christian tradition.

Note 4: "*Obscure merit of faith*": "The merit of faith consists in this, that man through obedience assents to things he does not see" (Thomas Aquinas, *Summa Theologica*, Part 3, Quest. 7, Art. 3).

86: *Meister Eckhart*'s (see editor's note for Ch. "Universal Categories", p. 61) saying, "*And the more man blasphemes, the more he praises God*" was among the articles for which he was charged with heresy, and which he himself subsequently revoked "insofar as they could generate in the minds of the faithful a heretical opinion" (The Bull, *In agro dominico* [1329]).

Degrees and Dimensions of Theism

90: For *the deist and Spinozan meaning* of "*pantheism*" see editor's note for Ch. "To Have a Center", p. 13.

The Sioux word *wakan*, the Algonquin *manitu*, and the Iroquois *orenda* are more or less synonymous, each referring to a spiritual power, or spiritual powers, belonging to a higher plane of reality but manifest in the world of space and time. Elsewhere the author writes, "It is true that the word 'spirit' is rather indefinite, but it has for that very reason the advantage of implying no restriction, and this is exactly what the 'polysynthetic' term *Wakan* requires" ("The Sacred Pipe", *The Feathered Sun: Plains Indians in Art and Philosophy* [Bloomington, IN: World Wisdom Books, 1990], p. 46). In the Japanese Shinto tradition, the term *kami* has almost exactly the same meaning, designating a mysterious sacred power, at once singular and plural, pervading the world and embodied in mountains, seas, rivers, rocks, trees, birds, animals, and extraordinary human beings.

"The *yogin* whose intellect is perfect contemplates all things as abiding in himself, and thus by the eye of knowledge he perceives that *everything is Ātmā*" (*Chāndogya Upanishad*, 6.1.4).

Note 2: John Toland (1670-1722) was a rationalist philosopher and "*free thinker*" whose works *deny the supernatural in religion.*

Note 3: *Paracelsus* (1493-1541) was a Swiss-German physician, botanist, astronomer, and esoterist.

93: For *Ashari* see editor's note for Ch. "Gnosis Is Not Just Anything", p. 55.

For *Ghazzali* see editor's note for Ch. "To Have a Center", p. 5.

"*God is one*": "Hear, O Israel: The Lord our *God is one* Lord" (Deut. 6:4); "Say: He *is God*, the *one*" (*Sūrah* "Purification" [112]:1).

Note 8: "*God doeth what He will*" (*Sūrah* "The Family of Imran" [3]:40 *passim*).

Isaiah was an eighth-century B.C. Jewish prophet whose writings are included in both the Jewish and Christian canons of the Bible.

Job was an ancient prophet whose story of personal affliction appears in both the Bible and the Koran.

Paul (c. 5-c. 67)—formerly Saul of Tarsus before his conversion to Christianity on the road to Damascus (see Acts 9:1-22)—was the Apostle to whom are attributed fourteen of the twenty-seven books of the New Testament.

94: For *Plato* see editor's note for Ch. "The Primacy of Intellection", p. 50.

The Hindu Trinity of the efficient Gods, Brahmā, Vishnu, and Shiva—respectively the creator, preserver, and transformer—is called the *trimūrti*, or "triple form".

Note 12: For *Maimonides* see editor's note for Ch. "Universal Categories", p. 77.

95: "*Made in the image of God*": "And God said, Let us make man in our image, after our likeness" (Gen. 1:26).

Although never defined as dogma, popular recognition of the Blessed Virgin as *Co-Redemptress* dates from ancient times and can be found in both the Eastern and the Western Churches; echoing the belief of many Christians, Saint Louis Marie de Montfort writes, "Let us boldly say with Saint Bernard that we need a mediator with the Mediator himself and that the divine Mary is the one most able to fulfill this office of love" (*True Devotion to the Blessed Virgin*).

The third of the Ecumenical Councils, meeting in Ephesus (431), declared that the Blessed Virgin Mary is rightly called the *Theotokos* or "*Mother of God*".

The Angelical Salutation, or "Hail Mary" (*Ave Maria*), in the Latin Rosary is: "Hail Mary, full of grace, the Lord is with thee; blessed art thou amongst women, and blessed is the fruit of thy womb, Jesus" (*Ave Maria gratia plena, Dominus tecum: benedicta tu in mulieribus, et benedictus fructus ventris tui, Jesus*) (cf. Luke 1:28, 42).

Note 14: In the author's original French, the word here rendered *Protestantism* is *Évangélisme* or "Evangelicalism", a term used in a European context to refer either to Lutheranism or to the union of the Lutheran and Reformed churches, or again to Protestant bodies in general.

"Our Father Who Art in Heaven"

97: "*Our Father who art in Heaven*" (Matt. 6:9; Luke 11:2).

98: *Rama* and *Krishna* are two of the ten *avatāras*, or incarnations, of the Hindu God Vishnu.

"Hail, thou that art highly favored [*full of grace*], *the Lord is with thee*: blessed art thou among women" (Luke 1:28); "For He hath regarded the low estate of His handmaiden: for, behold, from *henceforth all generations shall call me blessed*" (Luke 1:48).

For the Virgin Mary as "*Mother of God*" see editor's note for Ch. "Degrees and Dimensions of Theism", p. 95.

The *Immaculate Conception* is the Roman Catholic dogma that, from the first moment of her conception, Mary was free from all stain of original sin.

The *definition of the God-man*, including the relationship between Christ's *person* and *natures*, is discussed in great detail in the author's, "The Mystery of the Two Natures", in *Form and Substance in the Religions* (Bloomington, IN: World Wisdom, 2002).

Note 4: In the author's original French, the word here rendered *Protestantism* is *Évangélisme* or "Evangelicalism", a term used in a European context to refer either to Lutheranism or to the union of the Lutheran and Reformed churches, or again to Protestant bodies in general.

99: *Trinitarian theology* is discussed in greater depth in the author's, "Evidence and Mystery", in *Logic and Transcendence* (Bloomington, IN: World Wisdom, 2009), pp. 72-96.

100: "*The kingdom of God is within you*" (Luke 17:21).

101: "*But thou, when thou prayest, enter into thy closet, and when thou hast shut thy door, pray to thy Father, which is in secret*" (Matt. 6:6).

Hesychasts are monks of the Eastern Christian tradition whose aim is to attain to a state of *hesychia*, or inner stillness, through the practice of the Jesus Prayer, "Lord Jesus Christ, Son of God, have mercy on me, a sinner", also known as "the prayer of the heart". The author provides extended commentary on the invocation of the divine Name in various traditions in the chapter "Modes of Prayer", in *Stations of Wisdom* (Bloomington, IN: World Wisdom, 1995), pp. 121-145.

Note 8: *The injunction not to "utter vain words*": "But when ye pray, use not vain repetitions as the heathen do" (Matt. 6:7).

102: "No man speaking *by the Holy Spirit* calleth Jesus accursed" (1 Cor. 12:3).

"*Made in the image of God*": "And God said, Let us make man in our image, after our likeness" (Gen. 1:26).

Note 9: For *Meister Eckhart* see editor's note for Ch. "Universal Categories", p. 61.

David, Honen, Shankara

105: *David* (c. 1040-970 B.C.) was the second king of Israel and Judah, the composer of the *Psalms*, and, according to Christian tradition, an ancestor of Jesus Christ.

Honen Shonin (1133-1212), founder of the *Jōdo* or Pure Land school of Japanese Buddhism, taught that everyone without exception can be reborn into the "Pure Land" promised by the Buddha Amida simply by faithful repetition of Amida's Name.

Shankara (788-820), or *Shankaracharya*, was the foremost exponent of *Advaita Vedānta*, and considered by the author to be the greatest of all Hindu metaphysicians.

De profundis clamavi ad Te Domine is the Vulgate text of Psalm 130:1, "Out of the depths have I cried unto thee, O Lord".

Jesus is referred to as "*son of David*" on seventeen occasions in the New Testament, including the beginning of the Gospel of Matthew: "The book of the generation of Jesus Christ, the son of David. . ." (Matt. 1:1).

Note 1: The *Magnificat*, a hymn of praise sung by the Blessed Virgin after she had been greeted by her cousin Elizabeth as the mother of Christ, is thus named after the first word of the hymn in the Vulgate text: "And Mary said, My soul doth magnify the Lord [*Magnificat anima mea Dominum*]. And my spirit hath rejoiced in God my Savior. For He hath regarded the low estate of His handmaiden: for, behold, from henceforth all generations shall call me blessed. For He that is mighty hath done to me great things; and holy is His name. And His mercy is on them that fear Him from generation to generation. He hath shown strength with His arm; He hath scattered the proud in the imagination of their hearts. He hath put down the mighty from their seats, and exalted them of low degree. He hath filled the hungry with good things; and the rich He hath sent empty away. He hath helped His servant Israel, in remembrance of His mercy. As he spake to our fathers, to Abraham, and to his seed for ever" (Luke 1:46-55).

106: "Blessed is the man that walketh not in the counsel of the ungodly, nor standeth in the way of sinners, nor sitteth in the seat of the scornful. But *his delight is in the law of the Lord; and in his law doth he meditate day and night*" (Psalm 1:1-2).

"For *the Lord knoweth the way of the righteous; but the way of the ungodly shall perish*" (Psalm 1:6).

"*But know that the Lord hath set apart him that is godly for himself: the Lord will hear when I call unto him*" (Psalm 4:3).

For *Solomon* see editor's note for Ch. "Concerning an Onto-Cosmological Ambiguity", p. 82, Note 1.

107: *Solomon also had sanctuaries built for foreign divinities*: "Then did Solomon build an high place for Chemosh, the abomination of Moab, in the hill that is before Jerusalem, and for Molech, the abomination of the children of Ammon. And likewise did he for all his strange wives, which burnt incense and sacrificed unto their gods" (1 Kings 11:7-8).

The three Books of Solomon—Proverbs, Ecclesiastes, and the *Song of Songs*—have been interpreted by Jewish and Christian tradition as a spiritual ascent from purification to illumination to union.

Cabalists are Jewish mystics and esoterists.

For *Ramanuja* see editor's note for Ch. "The Primacy of Intellection", p. 49.

Vaishnavite monotheism refers to a form of Hindu *bhakti* characterized by devotion to the God Vishnu, whereas *Shaivite metatheism* refers to a form of non-dual Hindu *jnāna* connected with the God Shiva.

108: The *Brahma Sūtra*, one of the chief sources of Vedantic wisdom, traditionally attributed to the sage *Badarayana* (first century B.C.), distills and systematizes the teachings of the *Upanishads* concerning *Brahma*, the Supreme Reality.

"Brahma *alone is real; the world is illusion:* Māyā; *the soul is not other than* Brahma": this summation of *Advaita Vedānta* is traditionally ascribed to Shankara.

Nagarjuna (c. 150-250), founder of the *Mādhyamika* or "middle way" school of Buddhism and widely regarded in the *Mahāyāna* tradition as a "second Buddha", is best known for his doctrine of *shūnyatā*, or "emptiness", and for the correlative teaching that *Nirvāna* and *Samsāra* are essentially identical.

110: *Vasubandha*, a fourth century C.E. *Indian* monk and one of the founders of the Buddhist *Yogācāra* school, is recognized as a patriarch of both the *Jōdo* and Zen branches of Japanese Buddhism.

The "*Russian Pilgrim*" is the anonymous author of the nineteenth century Russian spiritual classic *The Way of a Pilgrim*, which extols the invocatory *method* of the Jesus Prayer (see editor's note for Ch. "Our Father Who Art in Heaven", p. 101).

Note 6: *Tan-Luan* (476-542), *Tao-Cho* (562-645), *Shan-Tao* (613-681), and *Genshin* (942-1017) are *patriarchs* of Amidism or "*devotional*" *Buddhism*, while *Kuya* (903-972) and *Ryonin* (912-985) were *Japanese precursors* of Honen.

111: *Faith* "*which moves mountains*": "If ye have faith as a grain of mustard seed, ye shall say unto this mountain, Remove hence to yonder place; and it shall remove; and nothing shall be impossible unto you" (Matt. 17:20).

Shinran (1173-1262), a *disciple of Honen* and founder of the *Jōdo-Shinshū* or "true pure land school" of Japanese Buddhism, rejected the "*way of merit*" and advocated complete reliance on the "*power of the other*" as manifest in the Name of the Buddha Amida, a single pronunciation of which is sufficient for rebirth in the Buddha's paradise, *Sukhāvatī*.

Fundamental Keys

113: "*Our Father who art in Heaven*, Hallowed be thy Name" (Matt. 6:9; Luke 11:2).

114: "*Made in the image of God*": "And God said, Let us make man in our image, after our likeness" (Gen. 1:26).

Note 4: *With the American Indians, the four universal Qualities are manifested mythically by the four cardinal points*: the cosmology and symbolic vocabulary of the American Plains Indians is lucidly exposited in the author's *The Feathered Sun: Plains Indians in Art and Philosophy*.

115: *Amore e'l cor gentil sono una cosa*—"Love and the noble heart are one thing"—is the first line of a poem in Dante's (see editor's note for Ch. "To Have a Center", p. 8) *La Vita Nuova*, "The New Life" (see editor's note for Ch. "To Have a Center", p. 15).

On the Art of Translating

119: "*There is nothing shameful in what is necessary for mortals*" is from Euripides' (see editor's note for Ch. "To Have a Center", p. 14, Note 20) play, *Antigone.*

120: *We do not accept that the words "rod" and "staff" in Psalm 23 are translated as "support" and "consolation"*: in the author's original French the respective terms are "*batôn*" *et* "*houlette*", and "*appui*" *et* "*consolation*".

Note 2: For *Dante* see editor's note for Ch. "To Have a Center", p. 8.

For *Shakespeare* see editor's note for Ch. "To Have a Center", p. 14, Note 20.

121: In the author's original French, "*to meditate*" is rendered as "*méditer*", and "*to whisper*" as "*murmurer*".

The Arabic formula rendered in French "may Allāh *pray on him and grant him a greeting*": the blessing upon the Prophet Muhammad is rendered "*que* Allâh *prie sur lui et lui accorde le salut*" in the author's original French.

For *Ave* and *Dominus tecum* see editor's note for Ch. "Degrees and Dimensions of Theism", p. 95.

"*Yo the believers*" is rendered "*ho les croyants*" in the author's original French.

122: *Le Petit Larousse* is a French-language encyclopedic dictionary that first appeared in 1905.

Gaius Julius *Caesar* (100-44 B.C.) was Roman Emperor from 49 B.C.

Marcus Tullius *Cicero* (106-43 B.C.) was a Roman statesman, philosopher, and orator.

123: *For "editing" as it is called in English*: the author uses the English term "*editing*" in the original French.

125: For *Aristotle* see editor's note for Ch. "To Have a Center", p. 20.

For *Meister Eckhart* see editor's note for Ch. "Universal Categories", p. 61.

127: "*Made in the image of God*": "And God said, Let us make man in our image, after our likeness" (Gen. 1:26).

Message of a Vestimentary Art

129: Note 1: *Jean Hani* (1917-2012) was a traditionalist author of works on Christianity, comparative religion, and symbolism. *La Divine Liturgie* ("The Divine Liturgy") was first published in French in 1981.

130: *The celestial Virgin who brought the sacred Pipe to the Red Indians* is *Pté-San-Win*, the White Buffalo Woman. A fuller account of this myth can be found in *The Sacred Pipe: Black Elk's Account of the Seven Rites of the Oglala Sioux* (1953), ed. Joseph Epes Brown.

Black Elk, or Hehaka Sapa (1863-1950), was a visionary holy man of the Oglala Indians who recounted his early life in *Black Elk Speaks* (1932), ed. John Neihardt.

131: Note 3: *Moeurs et Histoire des Indiens peaux-rouges* ("Customs and History of the Red Indians") by René *Thévenin and* Paul *Coze* was first published in Paris in 1928.

132: For *Vishnu* see editor's note for "Degrees and Dimensions of Theism", p. 94.

Note 4: *Lakshmi*, regarded in most traditions as the wife of Vishnu, is the Hindu goddess of good fortune and the embodiment of beauty.

134: For *Rousseau* see editor's note for Ch. "To Have a Center", p. 9.

James Fenimore *Cooper* (1789-1851) was the author of popular historical romances about Indian life and the American frontier; his best-known work is *The Last of the Mohicans.*

135: In the original French, the author has added the English term "*give away*" in parentheses after "fêtes de dons".

136: In the original French, the author uses the English phrase "*noble red man*".

Abd al-Rahman Ibn Muhammad *Ibn Khaldun* (1332-1402), a Muslim historian and philosopher, called attention to the recurrent conflict between nomadic and sedentary peoples in his *Kitāb al-ʿIbar*, "The Book of Examples [from the History of the Arabs and the Berbers]".

137: For *Lincoln* see editor's note for Ch. "To Have a Center", p. 25.

Concerning a Question of Astronomy

139: For *Ptolemy* see editor's note for Ch. "Universal Categories", p. 76.

Nicolaus *Copernicus* (1473-1543) formulated a heliocentric model of the universe in his work *De revolutionibus orbium coelestium* ("On the Revolutions of the Heavenly Spheres"), published just before his death.

Note 1: *Pythagoras* of Samos (b.c. 570 B.C.), an Ionian Greek philosopher, taught a metaphysics based upon the qualitative essence of numbers.

For *Aristotle* see editor's note for Ch. "To Have a Center", p. 20.

Anaximander (c. 611- c. 547 B.C.) was an early pre-Socratic philosopher who taught that all things are composed of *apeiron*, the "indefinite".

Aristarchus of Samos (c. 310-c. 230 B.C.) was a Greek astronomer and mathematician.

140: Note 2: For *Schiller* see editor's note for Ch. "To Have a Center", p. 13.

142: Note 4: Johannes *Kepler* (1571-1630) was a German astronomer and mathematician whose work primarily concerned planetary movements.

Selections from Letters and Other Previously Unpublished Writings

147: Selection 1: Letter of August 15, 1962.

For *Aristotle* see editor's note for Ch. "To Have a Center", p. 20.

Selection 2: Letter of January 31, 1996.

René *Guénon* (1886-1951), was a French metaphysician and prolific scholar of religions, one of the formative authorities of the perennialist school, and a frequent contributor to the journal *Études Traditionnelles.* His work *Orient et Occident* ("East and West") was published in 1924, the first English translation appearing in 1941. It was the first work in which Guénon elaborated a comprehensive critique of the modern West, later more fully developed in *La Crise du Monde Moderne* (1927) ("The Crisis of the Modern World") and *Le Règne de la Quantité et les Signes des Temps* (1945) ("The Reign of Quantity and the Signs of the Times").

For *Plato* see editor's note for Ch. "The Primacy of Intellection", p. 50.

Anaxagoras (c. 510-428 B.C.) was an Ionian pre-Socratic philosopher.

Protagoras of Abdera (c. 481-c. 411 B.C.) was a leading Sophist, known for his maxim that "man is the measure of all things".

Plotinus (c. 205-270), founder of the Neoplatonic school, endeavored to synthesize the teachings of Plato and Aristotle in his monumental *Enneads*, a collection of discourses compiled by his disciple Porphyry.

148: Selection 3: "Concerning the Article", unpublished, February 5, 1968.

Selection 4: Letter of January 17, 1976.

149: Selection 5: "The Book of Keys", No. 1158, "No Scissions in the Soul".

150: Selection 6: Letter of March 31, 1988.

Cain and Abel were the sons of Adam and Eve. Cain, a farmer, killed his brother, Abel, a shepherd (see Gen. 4:1-16).

"Woe unto the world because of offences! *for it must needs be that offences come*; but woe to that man by whom the offence cometh!" (Matt. 18:7).

The parable of the prodigal son is found in Luke 15:11-32.

Monica (331-387), the *mother* of *Augustine* of Hippo (see editor's note for Ch. "The Primacy of Intellection", p. 47), is said to have wept daily for the profligate life led by her son during the period before his conversion to Christianity.

Selection 7: Letter of September 18, 1953.

151: Selection 8: Letter of April 6, 1986.

For *Shankara* see editor's note for Ch. "David, Shankara, Honen", p. 105.

For *David* see editor's note for Ch. "David, Shankara, Honen", p. 105.

For *Honen* see editor's note for Ch. "David, Shankara, Honen", p. 105.

152: *Bernardino of Siena* (1380-1444), a priest and Franciscan missionary, was known as "the apostle of the Holy Name" because of his devotion to the *Name of Jesus.*

Selection 9: Letter of November 17, 1984.

153: Selection 10: Letter of April 1, 1985.

The "science of religions" or *Religionswissenschaft*, is the comparative and academic study of religions; the term was popularized by the German philologist and Indologist, Max Müller (1823-1900).

Selection 11: Letter of May 10, 1959.

Selection 12: "The Book of Keys", No. 502, "On the Spiritual Virtues".

154: Selection 13: Letter of June 9, 1982.

The *Buddha*'s "*Flower Sermon*" was a silent discourse in which he held up a white flower to signify the ineffable nature of *tathātā*, or "suchness". The origin of Zen Buddhism is attributed to this wordless teaching.

Selection 14: Letter of January 15, 1969.

155: Selection 15: Letter of May 6, 1978.

Selection 16: Letter of July 24, 1959.

156: Selection 17: Letter of October 5, 1977.

Selection 18: Letter of September 3, 1983.

157: Selection 19: Letter of September 3, 1983.

Lalla Yogishvari was a fourteenth century Kashmiri poet and saint; among the gems of her poetry, often quoted by the author, are the lines: "My guru spake to me but one precept. He said unto me, 'From without enter thou the inmost part.' That to me became a rule and a precept, and therefore naked began I to dance."

Selection 20: Letter of August 11, 1982.

Selection 21: "The Book of Keys", No. 220, "Specifications on the Question of the Ambience".

159: Selection 22: "The Book of Keys", No. 798, "*Pontifex* and *Khalīfah*".

"*He does not see the forest for the trees*" is a popular maxim to be found in several European languages, meaning that a preoccupation with details often obscures the larger picture.

GLOSSARY OF FOREIGN TERMS AND PHRASES

'Abd (Arabic): "servant" or "slave"; as used in Islam, the servant or worshiper of God in His aspect of *Rabb* or "Lord".

Ab intra (Latin): literally, "from within"; proceeding from something intrinsic or internal.

A contrario (Latin): literally, "from the opposite"; a form of argument in which a position is established or strengthened by highlighting the deficiencies of what opposes it.

Ad majorem Dei gloriam (Latin): "to the greater glory of God".

A fortiori (Latin): literally, "from greater reason"; used when drawing a conclusion that is inferred to be even stronger than the one already put forward.

A posteriori (Latin): literally, "from after"; subsequently; proceeding from effect to cause or from experience to principle.

A priori (Latin): literally, "from before"; in the first instance; proceeding from cause to effect or from principle to experience.

Adonai (Hebrew): Lord.

Advaita (Sanskrit): "non-dualist" interpretation of the *Vedānta*; Hindu doctrine according to which the seeming multiplicity of things is the product of ignorance, the only true reality being *Brahma*, the One, the Absolute, the Infinite, which is the unchanging ground of appearance.

Agathon (Greek): "the Good"; in Platonism, a name for the Supreme Reality.

Amore e'l cuor gentil sono una cosa (Italian): "Love and the noble heart are one thing"; a saying from Dante's *La Vita Nuova.*

Ānanda (Sanskrit): "bliss, beatitude, joy"; one of the three essential aspects of *Apara-Brahma*, together with *Sat*, "being", and *Chit*, "consciousness".

Apara-Brahma (Sanskrit): the "non-supreme" or penultimate *Brahma*, also called *Brahma saguna*; in the author's teaching, the "relative Absolute".

Ātmā or *Ātman* (Sanskrit): the real or true "Self", underlying the ego and its manifestations; in the perspective of *Advaita Vedānta*, identical with *Brahma.*

äußerst (German): "extremely" or "exceedingly".

Avatāra (Sanskrit): a divine "descent"; the incarnation or manifestation of God, especially of Vishnu in the Hindu tradition.

Ave (Latin): "Hail"; referring to the Angelical Salutation, or "Hail Mary" (*Ave Maria*) (cf. Luke 1:28).

Barakah (Arabic): "blessing", grace; in Islam, a spiritual influence or energy emanating originally from God, but often attached to sacred objects and spiritual persons.

Belle époque (French): "beautiful era"; the period of European history from the late nineteenth-century to the First World War.

Bhakti or *bhakti-mārga* (Sanskrit): the spiritual "path" (*mārga*) of "love" (*bhakti*) and devotion; see *jnāna* and *karma*.

Bon vivant (French): literally, "one who lives well"; a person who enjoys worldly pleasures, especially good food and drink.

Brahmā (Sanskrit): God in the aspect of Creator, the first divine "person" of the *Trimūrti*; to be distinguished from *Brahma*, the Supreme Reality.

Brahma or *Brahman* (Sanskrit): the Supreme Reality, the Absolute.

Brahma nirguna (Sanskrit): *Brahma* considered as transcending all "qualities", attributes, or predicates; God as He is in Himself; also called *Para-Brahma*.

Brahma saguna (Sanskrit): *Brahma* "qualified" by attributes and predicates; God insofar as He can be known by man; also called *Apara-Brahma*.

Brāhmana (Sanskrit): a member of the highest of the four Hindu castes; a priest or teacher.

Buddhi (Sanskrit): "Intellect"; the highest faculty of knowledge, distinct from *manas*, that is, mind or reason.

Chandāla (Sanskrit): an outcast or "untouchable"; someone outside the Hindu caste system.

Chintāmani (Sanskrit): the wish-fulfilling jewel; a symbol of the realized mind.

Chit (Sanskrit): "consciousness"; one of the three essential aspects of *Apara-Brahma*, together with *Sat*, "being", and *Ānanda*, "bliss, beatitude, joy".

Cinquecento (Italian): the Italian Renaissance of the sixteenth century, including in particular its art, architecture, literature, and music.

Cogito ergo sum (Latin): "I think therefore I am."

Corruptio optimi pessima (Latin): a scholastic axiom meaning, the "corruption of the best is the worst".

Creatio ex nihilo (Latin): literally "creation out of nothing"; a Semitic monotheistic dogma according to which God drew creation out of no pre-existent reality; often set in contrast to emanationist cosmogonies.

Cum grano salis (Latin): "with a grain of salt".

Darshan or *Darshana* (Sanskrit): a spiritual "perspective", point of view, or school of thought; also the "viewing" of a holy person, object, or place; more generally, the visual assimilation of celestial qualities or the contemplation of the Divine in nature or in art.

De facto (Latin): literally, "from the fact"; denoting something that is such "in fact", if not necessarily "by right".

De jure (Latin): literally, "by right"; an expression often used in contradistinction with *de facto.*

De profundis clamavi ad Te Domine (Latin): "Out of the depths have I cried unto thee, O Lord" (Ps. 130:1).

Deus sive natura (Latin): literally "God or nature"; a phrase associated with the Jewish philosopher Baruch Spinoza (1632-77), who used it to signify a single, ultimate reality.

Deva-yāna (Sanskrit): literally the "way of the gods"; the path followed by the faithful after death; may also mean a spiritual path.

Distinguo (Latin): literally, "I mark or set off, differentiate", often used in the dialectic of the medieval scholastics; any philosophical distinction.

Domine non sum dignus (Latin): "Lord, I am not worthy [that Thou shouldest come under my roof; but speak the word only and my soul shall be healed"]; spoken by the priest during the Tridentine Mass before communicating and before giving Communion to the people; cf. Matt. 8:8.

Dominus tecum (Latin): literally, "the Lord is with thee"; part of the Angelical Salutation, or "Hail Mary" (*Ave Maria*) (cf. Luke 1:28).

Eppur si muove (Italian): "And yet it moves"; uttered by Galileo when forced by the Inquisition to recant his heliocentric view that the earth moves around the sun.

Etude (French): literally, "study"; a short and technically difficult composition designed to develop a musician's skills.

Ex opere operato (Latin): literally, "from the work performed"; Christian teaching that divine grace is mediated through the sacraments by virtue of the corresponding rites themselves and independently of the merits or intentions of those by whom the rites are performed; in contrast to *ex opere operantis*, "from the work of the one working".

Hadīth (Arabic, plural *ahādīth*): "saying, narrative"; an account of the words or deeds of the Prophet Muhammad, transmitted through a traditional chain of known intermediaries.

Hic et nunc (Latin): "here and now".

Hypostases (Greek, singular, *hypostasis*): literally, "substances"; in Eastern Christian theology, a technical term for the three "Persons" of the Trinity; the Father, the Son, and the Holy Spirit are distinct *hypostases* sharing a single *ousia*, or essence.

Homo (Latin): "man"; referring to both the male and the female of the species; see *Vir*.

Homo faber (Latin): literally, "man the artisan"; man as creator or producer.

Homo religiosus (Latin): literally, "religious man"; the inherently religious nature of the human species.

Homo sapiens (Latin): literally, "wise man"; the human species.

Hyperdulia (Latin): reverence paid only to the Blessed Virgin; to be distinguished from *dulia*, the respect shown to saints.

Il dolce stil nuovo (Italian): "the sweet new style".

In divinis (Latin): literally, "in or among divine things"; within the divine Principle; the plural form is used insofar as the Principle comprises both *Para-Brahma*, Beyond-Being or the Absolute, and *Apara-Brahma*, Being or the relative Absolute.

In extremis (Latin): at the point of death; also, in grave or severe circumstances.

Ipso facto (Latin): by that very fact.

Īshvara (Sanskrit): literally, "possessing power", hence master; God understood as a personal being, as Creator and Lord; manifest in the *Trimūrti* as *Brahmā*, *Vishnu*, and *Shiva*.

Japa-Yoga (Sanskrit): method of "union" or "unification" (*yoga*) based upon the "repetition" (*japa*) of a *mantra* or sacred formula, often containing one of the Names of God.

Jinn (Arabic, singular *jinnī*): in Islam, creatures of fire, capable of changing size and shape, who can help or harm human beings.

Jiriki (Japanese): literally, "power of the self"; a Buddhist term for spiritual methods that emphasize one's own efforts in reaching the goal of liberation or salvation, as for example in Zen; in contrast to *tariki*.

Jīvan-mukta (Sanskrit): one who is "liberated" while still in this "life"; a person who has attained a state of spiritual perfection or self-realization before death; in contrast to *videha-mukta*, one who is liberated at the moment of death.

Jivātmā or *jivātman* (Sanskrit): literally, "the living self"; in Hindu tradition, the personal or individual soul associated with the physical body, as distinct from *Ātmā*.

Jnāna or *jnāna-mārga* (Sanskrit): the spiritual "path" (*mārga*) of "knowledge" (*jnāna*) and intellection; see *Bhakti* and *Karma*.

Jnānin (Sanskrit): a follower of the path of *jnāna*; a person whose relationship with God is based primarily on sapiential knowledge or *gnosis*.

Kami (Japanese): "deities", "spirits", and "energies" that pervade natural phenomena and which are worshipped in the Shinto tradition; may also refer to the spirits of the deceased.

Karma, *karma-mārga*, *karma-yoga* (Sanskrit): the spiritual "path" (*mārga*) or method of "union" (*yoga*) based upon right "action, work" (*karma*); see *Bhakti* and *Jnāna*.

Kategoria (Greek): "argument"; a key-notion capable of classifying other notions.

Khalīfah (Arabic, plural *khulafā'*): literally, "successor"; a representative or vicar, often used in reference to the successors of the Prophet Muhammad;

in Sufism, every man is in principle a *khalīfah* of God.

Kshatriya (Sanskrit): a member of the second highest of the four Hindu castes; a warrior or prince.

Latria (Latinized form of the Greek *latreia*): literally, "servitude, service"; the worshipful obedience owed only to God; to be distinguished from *dulia*, the respect shown to saints, and *hyperdulia*, the reverence paid to the Blessed Virgin.

Līlā (Sanskrit): "play, sport"; in Hinduism, the created universe is said to be the result of divine play or playfulness, a product of God's delight and spontaneity.

Mā shā'a 'Llāh (Arabic): "God has willed it".

Magnificat (Latin): literally, "doth magnify"; the song of praise sung by the Blessed Virgin Mary (Luke 1:46-55) when her cousin Elizabeth had greeted her as the mother of the Lord, so named from the opening word in the Vulgate: *Magnificat anima mea Dominum*, "My soul doth magnify the Lord."

Mahāyāna (Sanskrit): "great vehicle"; a form of Buddhism, including such traditions as Zen and *Jōdo-Shinshū*, regarded by its followers as the fullest or most adequate expression of the Buddha's teaching; distinguished by the idea that *Nirvāna* is not other than *samsāra* truly seen as it is.

Manitu (Algonquian Indian): spirit beings that reside in natural phenomena.

Mantra (Sanskrit): literally, "instrument of thought"; a word or phrase of divine origin, often including a Name of God, repeated by those initiated into its proper use as a means of salvation or liberation; see *Japa-yoga*.

Materia (Latin): literally, "material"; in Platonic cosmology, the undifferentiated and primordial substance that serves as a "receptacle" for the shaping force of divine forms or ideas; universal potentiality. Not to be equated with "matter" but rather with "substance" as pure potency.

Māyā (Sanskrit): universal illusion, relativity, appearance; in *Advaita Vedānta*, the veiling or concealment of *Brahma* in the form or under the appearance of a lower, relative reality; also, as "productive power", the unveiling or manifestation of *Ātmā* as "divine art" or theophany. *Māyā* is neither real nor unreal, and ranges from the Supreme Lord to the "last blade of grass".

Midrash (Hebrew): a corpus of rabbinical texts that interpret and explicate the Hebrew Scriptures.

Mudrā (Sanskrit): in the Hindu and Buddhist traditions, a ritual gesture usually made with the hands, but sometimes involving other parts of the body or the breathing; also a "seal" or "mark" of iconographical authenticity.

Mutatis mutandis (Latin): literally, "those things having been changed which need to be changed".

Namomitābhaya Buddhaya (Sanskrit): literally, "praise to Amida Buddha".

Namu-Amida-Butsu (Japanese): literally, "praise to Amida Buddha"; common formulation of the *nembutsu* in Pure Land Buddhism.

Nembutsu (Japanese): "remembrance or mindfulness of the Buddha", based upon the repeated invocation of his Name; same as *buddhānusmriti* in Sanskrit and *nien-fo* in Chinese.

Neti neti (Sanskrit): "not this, not this"; the apophatic negation of all qualities, attributes, or predicates relating to *Para-Brahma.*

Nirvāna (Sanskrit): literally, "blowing out"; in Indian traditions, especially Buddhism, the extinction of suffering and the resulting, supremely blissful state of liberation from egoism and attachment.

Nitya (Sanskrit): literally "eternal" or "timeless"; a pure spiritual state.

Noblesse oblige (French): literally, "nobility obliges"; the duty of the nobility to display honorable and generous conduct.

Nocturne (French): a musical composition inspired by or evoking night.

Orenda (Iroquois Indian): spirits or supernatural forces pervading natural phenomena.

Panchama (Sanskrit): "the fifth"; an outcast or person existing outside the Hindu system of four caste groups.

Para-Brahma (Sanskrit): the "supreme" or ultimate *Brahma*, also called *Brahma nirguna*; the Absolute as such; see *Apara-Brahma.*

Paraiyan (Tamil): literally, "tambourine man"; a pariah.

Paramātmā (Sanskrit): the "supreme" or ultimate Self; see *Ātmā.*

Perpetuum mobile (Italian): literally, "perpetual motion"; parts of music, characterized by a continuous steady stream of notes, to be played at rapid tempo; also, pieces of music to be played repeatedly or an indefinite number of times.

Philosophia perennis (Latin): "perennial philosophy".

Poètes maudits (French): literally, "accursed poets"; unrecognized poets living a dissolute life as social outsiders.

Pontifex (Latin): "bridge-maker"; man as the link between heaven and earth.

Prakriti (Sanskrit): literally, "making first" (see *materia*); the fundamental, "feminine" substance or material cause of all things; see *Purusha.*

Prapatti (Sanskrit): "seeking refuge"; pious resignation and devotion to God.

Princeps huius mundi (Latin): "prince of this world"; Satan, the devil.

Pro domo (Latin): literally, "for (one's own) home or house"; serving the interests of a given perspective or for the benefit of a given group.

Purusha (Sanskrit): "man"; the informing or shaping principle of creation; the "masculine" demiurge or fashioner of the universe, whose sacrifice gave rise to all creation.

Rabb (Arabic): "Lord"; in Islam, God in His aspect of Sovereign or Ruler; the divine complement of man as *'abd.*

Rahīm (Arabic): "the infinitely Merciful"; the beneficence of God insofar as it is directed toward men of good will; in Islam, one of the Names of God; see *Rahmān.*

Rahmah (Arabic): "compassion, mercy"; in Islam, one of the Names of God, who is supreme Compassion, Mercy, and Clemency.

Rahmān (Arabic): "the infinitely Good", "the Beneficent"; the compassion of God insofar as it envelops all things; in Islam, one of the supreme Names of God; see *Rahīm.*

Religio perennis (Latin): "perennial religion".

Rūh (Arabic): "breath, spirit"; in the Koran (*Sūrah "Al-Hijr*" [15]:29), the breath breathed into human beings by God to bring them to life.

Salla 'Llāhu 'alayhi wa-sallam (Arabic): "May God bless him and grant him peace"; a traditional formula of blessing upon the Prophet Muhammad.

Samādhi (Sanskrit): "putting together, union"; in Hindu *yoga*, a state of supreme concentration in which consciousness is entirely absorbed in the object of meditation.

Samsāra (Sanskrit): literally, "wandering"; in Hinduism and Buddhism, transmigration or the cycle of birth, death, and rebirth; also the world of apparent flux and change.

Sannyāsin (Sanskrit): "renunciate"; in Hindu tradition, one who has renounced all formal ties to social life.

Sat (Sanskrit): "being"; one of the three essential aspects of *Apara-Brahma*, together with *Chit*, "consciousness", and *Ānanda*, "bliss, beatitude, joy".

Shakti (Sanskrit): creative "power" or radiant "energy"; in Hinduism, expressed tantrically as the consort or feminine complement of Shiva.

Shūdra (Sanskrit): a member of the lowest of the four Hindu castes; a laborer.

Shuhūd (Arabic): "perception"; often in reference to the Sufi doctrine of *wahdat al-shuhūd*, "the unity of perception"; see *Wujūd*.

Shūnya (Sanskrit): "void" or "empty"; the absence of all definite being or selfhood; giving rise to the Buddhist concept of *Shūnyatā*, ultimate "emptiness", "voidness", or "suchness".

Sine qua non (Latin): an indispensable or essential condition.

Sirāt al-mustaqīm (Arabic): literally, "the straight path"; in the Koran, a group following an ascendant path on whom is God's favor; distinguished from those who go astray, and those on whom is God's anger (see *Sūrah* "The Opening" [1]:5-7).

Sophia Perennis (Greek): "perennial wisdom"; the eternal, non-formal Truth at the heart of all orthodox religious traditions.

Svarga (Sanskrit): heaven; in Hindu cosmology the celestial realm (*loka*) of Indra, situated on or above Mt. Meru.

Tale quale (Latin): "of such a kind as, as such".

Tao (Chinese): literally, "way"; in Taoism, the ultimate Source of all things, from which they come and to which they return; the Way of the universe and the sage.

Tariki (Japanese): literally, "power of the other"; a Buddhist term for forms of spirituality that emphasize the importance of grace or celestial assistance, especially that of the Buddha Amida, as in the Pure Land schools; in contrast to *jiriki*.

Theosis (Greek): "deification", participation in the nature of God (cf. 2 Pet. 1:4); in Eastern Christian theology, the supreme goal of human life; see *Deificatio.*

Trimūrti (Sanskrit): literally, "having three forms"; in Hindu tradition, a triadic expression of the Divine, especially in the form of Brahmā, the creator, Vishnu, the preserver, and Shiva, the transformer.

Upanishad (Sanskrit): literally, "to sit close by"; hence, any esoteric doctrine requiring direct transmission from master to disciple; in Hinduism, the genre of sacred texts that end or complete the *Vedas*; see *Vedānta.*

Upāya (Sanskrit): "means, expedient, method"; in Buddhist tradition, the adaptation of spiritual teaching to a form suited to the level of one's audience.

Vaishya (Sanskrit): a member of the third highest of the four Hindu castes; a craftsman, merchant, or farmer.

Varna (Sanskrit): caste; in Hinduism, the hierarchical division of society into four groups: *brāhmanas* (priests and teachers), *kshatriyas* (princes and warriors), *vaishyas* (merchants, farmers, and craftsmen), and *shūdras* (laborers).

Vedānta (Sanskrit): "end or culmination of the *Vedas*"; one of the major schools of traditional Hindu philosophy, based in part on the *Upanishads*, esoteric treatises found at the conclusion of the Vedic scriptures; see *Advaita.*

Vincit Omnia Veritas (Latin): "Truth conquers all".

Vir (Latin): "man"; the male of the species.

Wakan (Lakota Indian): "sacred" or "powerful".

Walī (Arabic): literally, "friend"; a saint.

Wujūd (Arabic): "being"; often in reference to the Sufi doctrine of *wahdat al-wujūd*, "the unity of being"; see *Shuhūd.*

Yā ayyuha 'lladhīna āmanū (Arabic): "O ye who believe"; a frequent refrain in the Koran in which God addresses the believers.

Yantra (Sanskrit): literally, "instrument of support"; a geometrical design, often representing the cosmos, used in Tantric Hinduism and Tibetan Buddhism as a visual support or focus for meditation.

Yin-Yang (Chinese): in Chinese tradition, two opposite but complementary forces or qualities, from whose interpenetration the universe and all its diverse forms emerge; *yin* corresponds to the feminine, the yielding, the moon, liquidity; *yang* corresponds to the masculine, the resisting, the sun, solidity.

Yoga (Sanskrit): literally, "yoking, union"; in Indian traditions, any meditative and ascetic technique designed to bring the soul and body into a state of concentration.

Yogin (Sanskrit): one who is "yoked or joined"; a practitioner of *yoga*, especially a form of *yoga* involving meditative and ascetic techniques designed to bring the soul and body into a state of concentration.

For a glossary of all key foreign words used in books published by World Wisdom, including metaphysical terms in English, consult: www.DictionaryofSpiritualTerms.org.
This on-line Dictionary of Spiritual Terms provides extensive definitions, examples, and related terms in other languages.

INDEX

BIOGRAPHICAL NOTES

Frithjof Schuon

Born in Basle, Switzerland in 1907, Frithjof Schuon was the twentieth century's pre-eminent spokesman for the perennialist school of comparative religious thought.

The leitmotif of Schuon's work was foreshadowed in an encounter during his youth with a marabout who had accompanied some members of his Senegalese village to Basle for the purpose of demonstrating their African culture. When Schuon talked with him, the venerable old man drew a circle with radii on the ground and explained: "God is the center; all paths lead to Him." Until his later years Schuon traveled widely, from India and the Middle East to America, experiencing traditional cultures and establishing lifelong friendships with Hindu, Buddhist, Christian, Muslim, and American Indian spiritual leaders.

A philosopher in the tradition of Plato, Shankara, and Eckhart, Schuon was a gifted artist and poet as well as the author of over twenty books on religion, metaphysics, sacred art, and the spiritual path. Describing his first book, *The Transcendent Unity of Religions*, T. S. Eliot wrote, "I have met with no more impressive work in the comparative study of Oriental and Occidental religion", and world-renowned religion scholar Huston Smith said of Schuon, "The man is a living wonder; intellectually apropos religion, equally in depth and breadth, the paragon of our time". Schuon's books have been translated into over a dozen languages and are respected by academic and religious authorities alike.

More than a scholar and writer, Schuon was a spiritual guide for seekers from a wide variety of religions and backgrounds throughout the world. He died in 1998.

Harry Oldmeadow was, until his recent retirement, the Coordinator of Philosophy and Religious Studies at La Trobe University Bendigo, in southeast Australia. A widely respected author on the *sophia perennis* and the perennialist school, his publications include *Traditionalism: Religion in the Light of the Perennial Philosophy* (2000) and *Frithjof Schuon and the Perennial Philosophy* (2010). He has edited several anthologies for World Wisdom, the most recent being *Crossing Religious Frontiers* (2010), and has contributed to such journals as *Sophia* and *Sacred Web*. In addition to his studies of perennialism, he has written extensively on the modern encounter of Eastern and Western traditions in works such as *Journeys East: 20th Century Western Encounters with Eastern Religious Traditions* (2004) and *A Christian Pilgrim in India: The Spiritual Journey of Swami Abhishiktananda* (2008).